Primary Initial Teacher Training and Education

Primary Initial Teacher Training and Education: Revised Standards, Bright Future?

Edited by Neil Simco and Tatiana Wilson

Learning Matters

The editors wish to acknowledge the support and encouragement of the National Primary Teacher Education Conference who, as the only organisation dedicated solely to primary teacher education, have a leading role in influencing the development of policy and practice in this area.

First published in 2002 by Learning Matters Ltd.

British Library Cataloguing in Publication Data
A CIP record for this book is available from the British Library.

ISBN 1 903300 52 5

Cover design by Topics – The Creative Partnership
Project management by Deer Park Productions
Typeset by PDQ Typesetting, Newcastle-under-Lyme
Printed and bound by Bell & Bain Ltd, Glasgow

Learning Matters Ltd
58 Wonford Road
Exeter EX2 4LQ
Tel: 01392 215560
Email: info@learningmatters.co.uk
www.learningmatters.co.uk

Qualifying to Teach: Professional Standards for Qualified Teacher Status and Requirements for Initial Teacher Training[1] was published earlier this year after a period of extensive consultation. The new Standards aim to streamline the Standards set out in Circular 4/98,[2] place a greater value on professional values and reflect recent developments in education. In addition the Standards broaden the range of degree subjects that could form an appropriate basis for entry to postgraduate initial teacher training, ensure that trainees are prepared to teach across a minimum of two Key Stages and no longer require primary trainees to train to teach a specialist subject.

One of the document's most welcome developments is that the Standards set out now cover all routes to Qualified Teacher Status, including flexible postgraduate initial teacher training and employment-based routes, thus offering a greater consistency of expectation for all newly qualified teachers entering the profession. As a result we have endeavoured to produce a book that is of relevance to all providers and partners involved in primary initial teacher training and education.

This book intends to provide an eclectic mix of practical advice and considered perspectives in relation to the new national framework. We hope to bring together the following three elements:

1. a constructive critique of the new Standards and requirements;
2. strategies and approaches to course design and assessment in order to meet the new requirements; and
3. a visionary section on the purpose and future direction of primary initial teacher training and education.

We also hope to create a forum for debate and for providers to share and disseminate good practice.

Summary and overview

Colin Richards, the current chair of the National Primary Teacher Education Conference (NaPTEC), introduces the book with his perspectives on the changes involved in the new requirements. He puts forward that becoming a primary school teacher is a more involved process than simply training and that novice teachers need to be educated as well as trained if they are to be able to become the reflective, responsive teachers of the future the profession needs. He argues there is a danger the Standards might present a view of emerging qualified teachers that is too limited whilst setting out a series of aims for initial teacher training and education for consideration.

The first two chapters are devoted to offering a broad range of perspectives on the new require-ments. The chapters are organised as essays considering to what extent and in what ways the new Standards will change for the better the education and training for the next generation of teachers. Responses are from different perspectives; a policy view and a view from a partnership school.

Chapter 3 considers inspection in initial teacher training and education. Jack Hogbin critiques the new Office for Standards in Education (OFSTED) regime within the sector and questions to what extent this represent a reliable, valid and transparent system of inspection. He puts forward that the relationship between new Standards and their interpretation by OFSTED remains key to their success in terms of providers offering creative and flexible courses, and calls for a public debate about the role of OFSTED, arguing that it is time for a change of culture.

Chapters 4 and 5 consider the new major emphasis in the new Standards on inclusion, and these chapters offers a critique on the rising profile of inclusion, including supporting pupils for whom English is an additional language. The chapters consider the potential of the new circular to shift expectations and practice in this key area and review a wide range of approaches to ensuring its realisation.

In Chapter 6 Phil Bassett discusses the role of partnership in initial teacher training. The new Standards establish and affirm the central importance of partnership in taking forward the revised requirements. This chapter offers a response to the broadening of the definition of partnership and includes a number of practical examples about how a range of provision has responded to the challenge of partnership. Bassett welcomes the reduction of Standards and hopes this will improve the experience of trainees. He points out some of the specific difficulties school-based providers will need to address and argues that effective partnership needs to be resourced adequately if the demands made on school-based training are to increase.

In Chapter 7, Simon Asquith discusses some proposals for strengthening the assessment for the award of Qualified Teacher Status (QTS). Reflecting this agenda, he disseminates a range of approaches which different providers are taking to reinforce current practice.

The new Standards no longer require a subject specialism. Mark Whitfield and Sandra Eady review the kind of teacher that *Qualifying to Teach* will encourage. Building on key arguments in Chapter 1, this chapter reviews a number of course designs that have responded in different ways to course requirements.

Section 3 of the book offers a vision of the future for initial teacher training and education. In Chapter 9 Neil Simco and Andrew Pollard begin with a review of the idea that a major purpose of initial teacher training and education is to meet the aspirations of society; this chapter goes on to develop a vision for what initial teacher training and education should look like by 2015. This is a wide-ranging, speculative account grounded in the reality of recent history and focuses on curriculum, pedagogy and policy. Finally, in Chapter 10, Denis Hayes considers what initial teacher training and education might feel like for the individual in 2015. Hayes offers two possible scenarios for the future and considers how these might be linked to teacher motivation and retention.

This book reflects the character of NaPTEC, which is widely regarded as an important voice for providers involved in the initial teacher training and education of primary teachers. We welcome all providers and partners involved in primary initial teacher training to join us and participate in our conferences, which are held twice a year.

We wish to acknowledge a number of people who have provided assistance in compiling this book. We are delighted that NaPTEC have been able to support this publication and hope that its fruition will provide a useful resource for the sector as it implements the new requirements. We would also like to acknowledge the work of Susan Cockburn in providing administrative support at an extremely busy time.

Neil Simco, St Martin's College and Tatiana Wilson, Exeter University
June 2002

1. Department for Education and Employment (DfEE) (1988) *Teaching: High Status, High Standards*. Circular 4/98. London: DfEE.
2. Department for Education and Skills (DfES) and Teacher Training Agency (TTA) (2002) *Qualifying to Teach: Professional Standards for Qualified Teacher Status and Requirments for Initial Teacher Training*. London: DfES/TTA.

Simon Asquith was Director of Undergraduate Initial Teacher Training at Liverpool Hope. In April 2002 he became Principal Lecturer (School Partnership Manager) at St Martin's College.

Phil Bassett is Head of the School of Education at North East Wales Institute and Chair of the Association for Partnerships in Teacher Education. He has taken a leading role in advising the TTA on the development of the new arrangements for partnership.

Christine Burns is currently the Team Leader for Primary English at the University of Exeter.

Stuart Calderbank is Assistant Headteacher of Claremont Primary School, Blackpool, and Joint Chair of the St Martin's College Primary Partnership Committee.

Sandra Eady is Principal Lecturer responsible for continuing professional development and research at St Martin's College, Carlisle campus.

Denis Hayes is Reader in Education at the Rolle School of Education, University of Plymouth. He takes a particular interest in the experiences of trainee primary teachers on school placement and the development of teaching expertise.

Jack Hogbin is Quality Adviser for the Faculty of Community Studies, Law and Education, at Manchester Metropolitan University. He has been in teacher education for more than 30 years and is a former Chair of the National Primary Teacher Education Conference (NaPTEC).

Andrew Pollard is Professor of Primary Education at Cambridge University and Director of the national Teaching and Learning Research Programme.

Colin Richards is a former senior HMI and is now Professor of Education at St Martin's College in Cumbria. Since 1999 he has been Chair of NaPTEC.

Neil Simco is Dean of Education at St Martin's College in Cumbria and Lancashire and has acted as consultant to the Teacher Training Agency.

Andrew Waterson is Senior Lecturer in the Education Department of St Martin's College.

Emma Westcott is a policy adviser to the General Teaching Council for England,. Her policy responsibilities encompass matters relating to entry to the profession, including recruitment, initial teacher training and induction. She is writing here in a personal capacity.

Mark Whitfield is Senior Lecturer and Programme Leader at St Martin's College, Carlisle campus, where he leads a major undergraduate programme within initial teacher training and education and where he is also responsible for primary information and comunication technology.

Teaching

> '... teaching involves a lot more than care, mutual respect and well-placed optimism. It demands knowledge and practical skills, the ability to make informed judgements, and to balance pressures and challenges, practice and creativity, interest and effort, as well as an understanding of how children learn and develop' (DfES/TTA, 2002, p. 4).

The knowledge, understanding, skills, attitudes and qualities required to be a primary school teacher have changed over time since the introduction of the pupil-teacher system in the century before last and during that time have been described in a wide variety of ways. This brief characterisation offered by the Department for Education and Skills (DfES) and the Teacher Training Agency (TTA) in their document on the revised Standards and requirements published in January 2002 provides a useful starting point from which to raise some important general issues which lie at the heart (and mind?) of being appropriately prepared to teach primary aged children.

Teacher training? Teacher education?

Accepting, provisionally, the DfES's and TTA's characterisation of what is involved in teaching, should initial teacher preparation be seen as a process of education or of training or of both? This is not just a peripheral semantic point. The language we use helps shape our view of the world and our place within it and informs the questions we ask, the assumptions we make and the actions we undertake. Crucially it also has a profound influence on how others see us. Language both reflects reality and shapes it.

It matters whether primary teachers are to be 'trained' or 'educated'. If they are to be 'trained' this implies they can be instructed systematically and unproblematically in the requirements of an occupation whose purposes are agreed and limited in number and scope, whose ways of proceeding can be specified mainly in behavioural terms, where scope for judgement is limited and where outcomes can be easily assessed, perhaps even 'measured'. If they are to 'educated' this implies they can be introduced in a justifiable but not necessarily systematic way to an occupation whose multiple purposes are contestable, whose ways of proceeding involve cognitive, affective as well as behavioural components, where a large element of judgement is required and where outcomes are uncertain and not necessarily measurable.

Teaching does have some elements that involve training. Would-be teachers can be (should be) trained to operate equipment; they can be trained in the techniques of black- or whiteboard writing; they can be trained in simple first-aid techniques; and so on. But referring to the quotation above can they be trained to 'make informed judgements'? Can they be trained to 'balance pressures and challenges'? Can they be trained to develop 'creativity'? Can they be trained in the values underlying such judgements? Clearly not. They need to be *educated* to make informed complex judgements; they need to be *educated* if they are to make balanced decisions; they need *educating* to appreciate the complex nature of teaching and learning if they are to be creative in the classroom; and they need to be *educated* in what professional values mean and involve. Jeffery (1946 p. 13), a former Director of the London Institute of Education, expressed it well over 50 years ago:

> *'Our very word "training" harbours a wrong idea about the teaching profession. You can train a dog, but you cannot train a teacher at least not in one year or in two years or in three. What you can do in three years, or in two, or even perhaps in one, is to give him* [sic] *some of the fundamental knowledge on which this craft is based and prepare him to learn what he can only learn in years of experience in the schools.'*

Becoming a primary teacher with the kinds of understanding and skills referred to in the opening quotation to this chapter involves a process of education and training (in that order) as recognised by Stuart Sutherland in his aptly named and sadly neglected report, *Teacher Education and Training: A Study* (1997). The TTA and the DfES need to rid themselves of the very limited and limiting view that while would-be teachers may need to be 'educated' in their subject studies they need only to be 'trained' in the task of teaching. They need to be 'educated' and to a lesser extent 'trained' in both. Neither of the terms 'student' or 'trainee' seems quite appropriate for would-be teachers; a new term altogether ('preparee' perhaps?) would be better! The new Standards and requirements are unfortunately still premised on the notion of training, despite the government's avowed intent to produce a 'world-class' education system. It is high time that the term 'teacher training' was buried; it has haunted teacher preparation for too long – limiting governments' views of what is required, limiting providers' views of their function and limiting would-be primary teachers' conceptions of what is required to be effective in the profession which they are proposing to enter.

The aims of teacher education and training

Through a list of what it terms 'Standards' the document published in January 2002 specifies the professional values, the practical skills, the knowledge and (to a lesser extent) the understanding required of 'those awarded qualified teacher status', though thankfully not in quite the highly detailed, prescriptive tone of its predecessor, Circular 4/98 (DfEE, 1998). It itemises, too, the requirements to be made of providers in relation to trainee (*sic*) entry requirements, training and assessment, management of the initial teacher training (ITT) school partnership and quality assurance. Unlike Circular 4/98 it does not prescribe a curriculum but like its predecessor it fails to provide an explicit statement of the aims underlying the enterprise of teacher preparation though, to be fair, it does go a little way to providing this indirectly through its valuable characterisation of teaching (reproduced in part at the beginning of this chapter).

An explicit statement of aims would give a firmer sense of direction to providers as they plan and transact their courses. It would provide a justification (albeit inevitably a contestable one) for the detailed outcomes expected of those awarded qualified teacher status (QTS). It would help stimulate an important debate on the future of teacher education and training. It would provide clearer criteria against which courses could be appraised or inspected. For example, without explicit reference to aims, judgements that institutions *x* and *y* are 'high quality' providers will mean nothing, apart from conveying a general sense of approval by the Office for Standards in Education (OFSTED) and theTTA. Equally, judgements of the effectiveness of courses are empty unless it is clear what aims are being effectively achieved (see Richards, 2001).

The National PrimaryTeacher Education Conference (NaPTEC) has long been of the view that circulars or other official documentation setting out the content or the outcomes of teacher education and training should be set within as clear and as agreed a view as possible of the aims of the enterprise. Such a view might, for example, include statements to the effect that courses of ITT should ensure that students (preparees?):

- have a strong sense of professional values which they embody in their work;
- develop the understanding, knowledge and skills necessary for achieving high academic Standards in their subject(s) or areas of study;
- develop the ability to translate the knowledge they have of subjects or areas of study into terms that children of primary-school age can understand (pedagogic subject knowledge);
- demonstrate an understanding of the wide variety of ways in which children learn and can apply that understanding in the skilful employment of different methods of teaching;
- think openly, rigorously and critically about policies and practices related to teaching, learning, curriculum and assessment;
- begin to develop their own vision of what constitutes an effective practitioner;
- engage with other professional perspectives on the upbringing of children;
- are offered access to, and critiques of, inspection and other evidence-based research;
- become practitioners committed to their own as well as pupils' learning;
- understand and critically engage with the thinking informing recent developments in education at national level; and
- are constructively critical of their own professional preparation.

Taking these as embodying criteria against which to be judged, how do the new Standards bear up to scrutiny?

The new Standards: an appraisal

Professional values and practice

Commendably, the first set of Standards relate to *Professional values and practice* (based on the General Teaching Council's professional code). The values embodied in the Standards are very important even if they are non-contentious: valuing and respecting persons and their backgrounds; care and concern for their development; recognition of others' rights, responsibilities and interests; commitment to inclusion and educational achievement; and commitment to professional development and improvement. The practices include effective communication with parents, carers and other professionals and contribution to the corporate life of schools. In part, then, the new Standards do embody the first of the purposes listed above.

For the purposes of assessment the values are not without their problems. They may be non-contentious at an abstract level but controversy is likely to arise over how 'preparees' can demonstrate to the satisfaction of others (including OFSTED inspectors) that they understand, uphold and demonstrate these in practice.

But is the list of values and practices complete? Why, for example, is there nothing along the lines of 'a constructive and, where necessary, critical awareness of national policies affecting the education service '? Or no reference along the lines of 'a commitment to a thoughtful and sensitive implementation of national and school policies'? Why nothing on 'a willingness to innovate in a considered, sensitive way'? Why no reference to any 'personal vision of teaching and learning '? The DfES and TTA aim to produce caring, concerned, respectful teachers anxious to promote inclusion and educational achievement but only in ways fully congruent with current government thinking. Compliance seems to be the underlying (though implicit) value – a far cry from the value of 'criticality' espoused by a generation of teacher educators or from the value of 'freedom' espoused by successive generations of teachers after the Second World War and memorably expressed by a Senior Chief Inspector of Schools half a century ago: *'freedom of thought, of action and, above all, of judgement; not freedom as a right, not freedom to rule and direct; but freedom as a solemn duty, freedom to serve and collaborate'* (Roseveare, 1950, p. 14). The values implicit in, or missing altogether from, the new statement of Standards are far more contentious than those listed, but will 'preparees' be made aware of them and of their importance to some conceptions of what constitutes ' good', 'effective' or 'professional' teaching?

Overall, in their treatment of values the Standards only partially reflect the purposes outlined above. They are necessary but, arguably, not sufficient as a basis for responsive, yet reflective teacher professionalism.

Knowledge and Understanding

The standards related to 'Knowledge and Understanding' focus on subject knowledge per se and on knowledge of 'official' requirements. Circular 4/98's (DfEE, 1998) obsession with the minutiae of subject knowledge is replaced by a more sensible and defensible acknowledgement of its important place in initial teacher preparation along with non-statutory examples of knowledge, understanding and skills which are intended to help providers plan their courses and to help in the assessment of preparees. The importance of ensuring that these examples remain non-statutory cannot be overestimated if providers are to exercise the professional judgement the TTA claims to want to foster.

In the wording of the Standards there is surprisingly little explicit reference to the significance of pedagogic subject knowledge through which subject knowledge is mediated to children in terms they can understand and connect with. There is also only limited reference to the importance of an understanding of how children learn, develop and make their own sense of what is taught – one Standard only and not accorded prominence.

The concept of mediation is also missing in relation to preparees' knowledge and understanding of 'official' requirements. There are plentiful and appropriate references to national statutory requirements, national frameworks, national assessment and reporting arrangements and principles set out in national guidance. Certainly, would-be teachers need to know and understand what is statutory but they also need the ability (and encouragement) to apply nationally enunciated principles related to inclusion, assessment and learning sensitively to the contexts in which they teach. The DfES and TTA fail to acknowledge that the kind of 'informed judgements' referred to at the very beginning of this chapter require the skilful application of principles mediated by knowledge of the circumstances in which they have to be applied.

The other missing dimension to this section is any understanding of how and why these statutory requirements, frameworks, etc., have been developed (and changed over time) and any indication that they are contestable, that they could be different and that they could be (and are being) challenged in some quarters. If they are to make sense of the demands made on the teaching profession and judge their appropriateness, preparees need a sense of context that a critical study of the recent history of primary education can provide.

In its treatment of knowledge and understanding the new document is a marked improvement on its dirigiste predecessor but it only goes some way to meeting the criteria embodied in the purposes in the third section of this chapter.

Teaching

The Standards in the 'Teaching' section relate to: 1) planning, expectations and targets; 2) monitoring and assessment; and 3) teaching and class management. These are fewer in number than those in Circular 4/98. As general statements most are appropriate and non-contentious but as with the professional values previously discussed the difficulty lies in how they are operationalised and assessed – matters needing to be left to the professional judgement of providers (working in partnership with teachers in schools and in association with, but not dominated by, OFSTED inspectors?).

The Standards related to planning are sensible and realistic. Others concerned directly with the act of teaching embody an appropriate, eclectic view of teaching strategies and avoid Circular 4/98's preoccupation with the setting of tasks for, and teaching of, 'whole classes'. This more liberal view is epitomised by the inclusion as part of a Standard of a requirement anathema to the spirit and letter of Circular4/98 i.e. that those awarded Qualified Teacher Status should demonstrate that they *promote active and independent learning that enables pupils to think for themselves, and to plan and manage their own learning*. Unfortunately within the Standards there is no explicit requirement for preparees to study the strengths and weaknesses of a variety of teaching methods as discussed in research and other professional literature.

The Standards relating to monitoring and assessment are realistic in the current national context but betray a different kind of obsession – the DfES's preoccupation with testing, assessment and the use of school and classroom data on pupil attainment. There is no encouragement in the circular for would-be teachers to think openly, rigorously and critically about assessment policy and practice and their effects on teaching, learning and teachers' and children's self-esteem.

Raising, changing the standard?

The new Standards and requirements are an improvement on those in Circular 4/98. They are more concise, have a clearer structure and are more manageable. The new Standards are no less rigorous but are more easily (though not easily!) assessable. They embody a 'less illiberal' view of initial teacher education and training, though still with an emphasis on the latter. More has been left to the professional judgement of providers.

However, as this chapter has pointed out, the new Standards and requirements do have a number of shortcomings in relation to the view of teacher education and training NaPTEC would advocate. In summary, its view of the emerging qualified teacher is too limited.

An analogy with medicine may help, though admittedly analogies inevitably break down at some point. It is clear from the content of the revised documentation that its authors are not setting out to prepare the educational equivalent of medical technicians – following closely prescribed rules and procedures with very limited room for discretion and working under the tight control of others. But neither are they intent on preparing the educational equivalent of medical practitioners operating within professionally derived guidelines and codes of practice, employing sophisticated skills and judgement, enjoying a very large measure of judgement and discretion and operating in clinical matters without intervention from non-medical sources. The new Standards and requirements seem to be concerned with the preparation of skilled educational 'paramedics' – with considerable room for discretion and practical judgement but *only* within strict (in this case government-controlled) limits and policies which are not seen as open to critical scrutiny, mediation and adaptation by those entering, or in, the teaching profession. Compared with Circular 4/98 the new document has changed, perhaps even raised, the standard expected of providers and preparees, but not to the extent required if the government's vision of recruiting and retaining a 'world-class' teaching force is to be realised.

References

Department for Education and Employment (DfEE) (1998) *Teaching: High Status, High Standards.* Circular 4/98. London: DfEE.

Department for Education and Skills (DfES) and Teacher Training Agency (TTA) (2002) *Qualifying to Teach: Professional Standards for Qualified Teacher Status and Requirements for Initial Teacher Training.* London: DfES/TTA.

Jeffery, G. (1946) *The Service of a Great Profession.* London: National Union of Teachers.

Richards, C. (2001) *School Inspection in England: A Reappraisal. Impact 9.* London: Philosophy of Education Society of Great Britain.

Roseveare, M. (1950) *Age, Aptitude and Ability.* London: National Union of Teachers.

Sutherland, S. (1997) *Teacher Education and Training: A Study. Report 10 of the National Committee of Inquiry into Higher Education.* London: HMSO.

Section 1:
Qualifying to teach: a critique of the new Standards and requirements

The establishment of the General Teaching Council

The General Teaching Council (GTC) for England was established by the Teaching and Higher Education Act 1998 as an independent professional body for teaching and began work in autumn 2000. A council with similar powers and duties was established for Wales at the same time. The Act concluded over 150 years during which teachers and teacher educators had pressed for such a body, latterly with support from the broader community of interest in teaching (including unions, parents, governors and employers) under the aegis of the GTC (England and Wales) Trust.

The legislation bringing the Council into being provided for a wide-ranging regulatory and advisory role, but the powers fell short of the aspirations of campaigners for such a body. Many of those who advocated that teaching should become self-regulating expected the profession to be entrusted with setting entry standards, as well as presiding over exit from the profession through hearings relating to competence and conduct. It has been suggested that the profession cannot be described as self-regulating without the demonstration of such trust.

Nevertheless, a sense of realpolitik characterised the campaign for a council, which carefully included a 'best case scenario' in which the council set entry standards and requirements for programmes of initial teacher training (ITT), and – in the event of Ministers declining to cede their powers in this area – a model in which the council was the key source of ministerial advice on these matters.

The passage of the Teaching and Higher Education Bill through Parliament included many heated debates on the extent of the Council's powers, with a particular focus on powers to define standards for the award of Qualified Teacher Status (QTS) and ITT requirements. Members of both houses had been involved in earlier pushes for a general teaching council and had more than a lay command of the arguments. They were also familiar with the more substantial powers of the Scottish GTC, which had existed since 1966, and they sought similar powers for its English and Welsh counterparts.

Assurances were given at various stages of the bill process that the government envisaged taking an incremental approach to the accretion of powers by the Council. The effective discharge of its 'start-up' powers, it was suggested, would strengthen the case for new powers in due course. Baroness Blackstone was charged with steering the passage of the bill through the Lords' stages. In response to probing from the Lords Preston, Glenemara and Tope, she cautioned:

'We must approach this matter with care. We must build. It may well be that in ten years' time the final shape of the General Teaching Council will be rather different from what it is when established … It may start with a slightly more limited remit compared to its eventual remit' (Hansard, 1396, cited in Sayer, 2000).

When the bill was enacted, the Council was given advisory powers in relation to teacher training and standards of teaching, and the Secretary of State was required to consult the GTC over changes to the QTS or induction Standards, in recognition of their significance for the integrity of the council's register. The Council has now assumed responsibility for the award of QTS, but only in an administrative sense – the power to define the basis of the award remains with the Secretary of State.

The review of the existing circular

When the Council started its work, the framework for ITT was laid out in Circular 4/98 (DfEE, 1998), a circular that had continued the trend towards prescription of the ITT curriculum and that had included for the first time a 'national curriculum for ITT' in the core subjects. Many ITT providers were alarmed about increasing prescription and about the apparent separation of competence-based outcomes from a rich diet of what has been termed 'practical theorising' in ITT provision (Furlong, 2000). Teachers engaged with 'practical theory' might be described as having the skills, opportunity and commitment to subject practice to conceptual and analytical scrutiny in the pursuit of the greater understanding without which improvement is impossible.

In its favour, the circular did have the merit of achieving greater clarity about what the 'consumers' of ITT were due. The Council has expressed the view that professional entry Standards need to be known and understood by teachers. Circular 4/98 provided a clear expression of what could be expected of a newly qualified teacher that made it more widely used in schools than its predecessors.

However, the circular also had that particular built-in obsolescence that can befall statutory documents conceived under one administration and implemented by the next. Some of the ideological leanings of the *ancien régime* were embedded in 4/98. The QTS Standards evoke an understanding of teaching as the skilful imparting of knowledge, particularly subject knowledge. No one would deny this was an important element in the repertoire of the effective teacher. However, the circular gives teaching and learning the character of purely technical transactions rather than social acts, and there is little reference to the context of teaching and learning. Pupils are neutral vessels into which teachers decant what they know. There are few references to factors that may influence this process, such as race, gender, class or disability status. It is interesting to compare, for example, the minimal references to race in 4/98 with the references in the induction Standards devised shortly after for the Labour Secretary of State. The induction Standards were produced for a different government, but also in the context of the Macpherson inquiry (1999) into the police handling of the racist murder of the black teenager, Stephen Lawrence. Recent cohorts training under 4/98 have only had to know about the Race Relations Act (1976) in order to meet the QTS requirements, yet a year into their professional practice they are expected to factor race and English language acquisition into individual pupil planning; to use ethnic and cultural diversity to enrich the curriculum and raise achievement; and to implement school policies on harassment. This highlights the need for better coherence between Standards relating to different professional phases.

Circular 4/98 came into force for trainees embarking on ITT from the autumn of 1998. The Green Paper published that autumn, *Teachers: Meeting the Challenge of Change,* made it clear that the Labour government was taking a comprehensive view of the levers for reform of the teaching profession, and that the Secretary of State's power over entry to the teaching profession was viewed as a significant lever. The Green Paper carried proposals for testing trainees' knowledge of literacy, numeracy and information and communication technology (ICT), and strengthening assessment against the QTS Standards. It seemed only a matter of time before the Secretary of State would take the opportunity to ensure that the framework for ITT reflected his government's priorities for education.

In December 1999 the Secretary of State announced a review of the existing QTS Standards and ITT requirements to be undertaken by the Teacher Training Agency (TTA). The review was to begin with an extensive monitoring period during which the agency conducted a very thorough trawl of stakeholder views of the existing circular. The Council came into being when this monitoring phase was well advanced. Members of the Council's ITT Advisory Committee decided to issue some early advice on the review, to disseminate initial thinking and solicit reactions, and to press for a particular stake in the next stage of the process (the full text of this and other advice is available from the Council's website at www.gtce.org.uk).

The Council wanted to contribute to, but not be confined to, the terms of the review underway. Its advice touched on other issues, from the challenges of diversity to the support and recognition afforded teacher educators in schools. This chapter takes the QTS Standards as its main focus, but the Council will want to give equal attention in forthcoming years to the ITT requirements – the characteristics of the framework within which new entrants to the profession work towards entry Standards. The Council's two contributions to the review of Circular 4/98 begin to advance perspectives and articulate some concerns in this area.

Key themes of the Council's early advice

A simpler, more coherent set of Standards

There was unanimity among teacher educators in schools and higher education institutions (HEIs) about the need for a more coherent and streamlined set of QTS Standards. The then Minister for School Standards, Estelle Morris, confirmed at an early stage in the review that this message had been heard, and the TTA was asked to ensure that the replacement circular had leaner statutory requirements. The Council had no difficulty in supporting the sector's views, believing that over-prescription could make the providers' approach to important areas for development rather mechanistic, and fewer key foci would result in a better learning experience.

Enabling new teachers to contribute to social and educational inclusion

The Council's early discussions with teachers revealed a great deal of support among teachers for the government's emphasis on tackling underachievement and disengagement, but a widespread concern that teachers are not adequately supported to make a positive contribution to this agenda. In particular, they highlighted poor access to the expertise of other professionals and inadequate professional development opportunities with regard to social inclusion. The agency's annual survey of new teachers asks how well prepared they feel for aspects of their work, and new teachers often feel insufficiently prepared to support pupils with special educational needs and ethnic minority pupils, particularly those who have English as an additional language. Their concerns about behaviour management can also be assumed to relate to pupils with emotional and behavioural difficulties and others who are disengaged from learning. The Council advised that ITT (and subsequent professional development opportunities) should better equip new teachers to contribute to social and educational inclusion. These themes have been strengthened in the revised Standards. Moreover, the teacher's commitment to working with other professionals in the pupil interest is an aspect of the GTC's professional code and the new Standards relating to values and practice.

More about the values that underpin good teaching

Teaching is a social act requiring more than skills and knowledge – teachers told us that Circular 4/98 promoted a conception of teaching as technical competence, 'decoupled' from the values, ethics and commitments that support effective teaching. Teachers wanted trainees to be exposed to and involved in the dialogue that had informed their professional formation as new teachers, and to be immersed in debates about the ethical, moral and social commitments involved in teaching.

It goes without saying that professional values are difficult to define, let alone to teach. Even if it is possible to devise a form of words to express a value, it may be interpreted differently by colleagues in the same profession, and even in the same school. However, it seemed better to attempt to include professional values, and risk doing so clumsily, than to omit any reference to them at all. The Council expressed the view that while there were philosophical and practical difficulties associated with assessing trainees' values *per se*, it was possible to check for behaviours and practices that might flow from particular values and commitments.

In addition to arguing for a strong focus on professional values, the Council took the view that teachers themselves were best placed to define, from their experience, what one needed beyond skills and knowledge to be a good teacher. This was exactly the process behind the development of the Council's first professional code for teaching, which had been published in draft form for consultation. The Council made the following pitch:

> *'Now that teachers have a professional body, it is for the profession itself to define the values that underpin teaching, not least through the development of a professional code for teachers ... A statement of values which is devised by and for the profession*

is likely to be better regarded and thus more effective than a statement prepared for the profession by others' (GTCE, 2000).

In the fullness of time, the Council would like to fulfil the aspirations of those who campaigned for a professional body for teaching and define the professional entry Standards it upholds through its regulatory roles. In the interim, it seemed highly appropriate to entrust the profession with devising Standards relating to professional values. Fortuitously, Estelle Morris agreed and asked the Council to work with the TTA on a set of Standards derived from its professional code. For the Council, this represented a significant first step in its work on professional standards. It also provided the opportunity to embed the Council's code and, by implication, the Council, in the consciousness of every new teacher.

The resulting Standards sit at the start of *Qualifying to Teach* (DfES/TTA, 2002), and expectations in terms of knowledge and understanding, and teaching, flow from the professional values and commitments of the teacher. Broadly speaking, they reflect the themes of the Council's first professional code. There are a couple of differences of emphasis worth noting as a means of illustrating the complexity of the task and of highlighting some of the Council's interests for the future.

First, Standard 1.5 (DfES/TTA, 2002) requires trainees to demonstrate that *'They can contribute to, and share responsibly in, the corporate life of schools.'* This is a valuable standard in its own right, as it provides an opportunity to ensure that trainees understand that education is a collective endeavour, and the effectiveness of formal and informal learning a collective responsibility. However, the Council's interest here went beyond the community of the school, and into the communities served by the school. The professional code (GTCE, 2002) asserts that *'Teachers support the place of the school in the community.'*

New teachers should understand that (most) schools are community resources, and that the community can be a resource for the school. They need to know that they have a responsibility to glean enough about the context in which the school operates to deliver effective learning opportunities in that context, and respond as appropriate to local circumstances and events through their work.

Secondly, Standard 1.7 (DfES/TTA, 2002) requires trainees to demonstrate that:

> *'They are able to improve their own teaching, by evaluating it, learning from the effective practice of others and from evidence. They are motivated and able to take increasing responsibility for their own professional development.'*

Again, this is a fair reflection of what is in the Council's professional code (GTCE, 2002) about teachers' commitment to their own professional development and to learning from colleagues. However, the code places significant emphasis on teachers *teaching* their colleagues as well as learning from them. The code (ibid.) affirms that:

'Teachers support their colleagues in achieving the highest professional standards. They are fully committed to sharing their own expertise and insights, in the interests of the people they teach.'

Teachers are, increasingly, people who teach adults as well as children and young people. They are routinely involved in the professional development of teaching and other colleagues. As trainee mentors, induction tutors and participants in performance management, teachers are required to utilise skills in peer tutoring, mentoring and coaching in addition to some of the pedagogic skills they deploy every day in support of children's learning. The Council believes this professional expertise should be recognised and supported from the outset of a career in teaching, because it is becoming a core aspect of teachers' professionalism. It also underpins the government's strategy for teachers' continuing professional development, which places an emphasis on the need to increase effective learning opportunities within and between schools.

It might be suggested that recognition of this aspect of teachers' work would make a career in teaching more attractive to some potential recruits. There are certainly many serving teachers who have explicitly chosen the professional development of colleagues as their area of specialism over management or curriculum responsibilities. The Council's draft *Professional Learning Framework* (2001) (issued for consultation at the time of writing) contains a section dedicated to teachers' involvement in the development of their colleagues' practice, which includes the following observations:

'Recognition for this area of professional practice has been low with few training op-portunities or accredited programmes to develop the skills required. It is through these roles that teachers take on increasing 'pedagogical leadership'. ITT and induction should also enable less experienced teachers to have an impact on the learning of their more experienced colleagues. Recognition of this two-way benefit is a key part of the new Early Professional Development programme [being piloted by the Department for Edu-cation and Skills on the Council's advice].'

Teachers who support trainees in schools have told the Council that this is a feature of, and rationale for, their involvement in ITT. ITT providers have also confirmed that they make use of activities such as peer mentoring and tutoring, team teaching and lesson feedback that enable trainees to begin to develop the skills, knowledge and commitment to support the development of colleagues.

The Council will seek to promote and build this aspect of teacher professionalism through its contribution to the development of the rest of the professional Standards framework. It will be important, for example, to make sure that, in future, induction develops the new teachers' capacity for supporting the development of colleagues.

Conclusions

The Council has praised the thoroughness of the TTA's work in developing *Qualifying to Teach* (DfES/TTA, 2002), and its small involvement has provided an insight into the complexity of setting Standards and the skills and sensitivities involved. For the main part, the Council's aspirations for the new Standards were readily accommodated – not least because they reflected accurately a broad consensus about how the Standards might be improved. A few of the points at which the Council view departed from the prevailing view have been highlighted here in order to provide an insight into the particular emphases and aspirations of a new body involved for the first time in a review of Standards for the award of QTS.

If it is not unwise to pronounce on the magnitude of a shift in policy before it is implemented, it seems fair to say that *Qualifying to Teach* represents a small but significant step towards genuine professional entry Standards for teaching.

The Council's professional code (GTCE, 2002) represents a collective professional view of some of the principal characteristics of teaching professionalism, and that view will now shape all ITT. Some view the code as 'motherhood and apple pie', and its contents can seem anodyne until one considers how far we are from providing an environment in which all teachers have the training and support to match their own high expectations and aspirations for professional practice. 'Standard-ese' is a dry language, and some of the power of the values expressed in the code may have been dissipated in the process of translation into the language of Standards. However, it is still possible to envisage a range of exciting and challenging learning activities flowing from a critical exploration of the teacher's relationships with and commitments to pupils, parents, communities, teaching colleagues and other colleagues, within and beyond the school. Central to the transmission, critical engagement and absorption of professional values is the dialogue between trainees with a wide range of backgrounds and prior experiences, and equally diverse teacher educators in schools and HEIs. The process is arguably as important for the health of the profession as the outcomes.

It would be foolish to suggest that this modest step has quickened the hearts of most teachers, or even that ownership of professional Standards is yet among the key concerns that teachers want the Council to address. The fact that some (but not all) teachers are unaware of, and indifferent to, debates about the provenance of professional Standards could be viewed as one area for 'baseline assessment' for a new professional body, on the standing of the profession. If the Council can ensure that the professional Standards framework has a resonance with teachers and translates into entitlements to personal, professional and career development, perhaps teachers in future will view these debates as critical to their professional identity and standing.

The Council has started its work at a time when the very notion of a 'profession' is contested. It has been argued that there is no fixed definition of a profession and that claims to 'professionalism' are always influenced by the contemporary political and economic climate (Ozga, 1997). Such commentators express dubiety about the external and internalised pressures placed upon occupational groups by notions of professionalism. Others would argue that it is possible to identify common characteristics of occupational groups deemed professional, and that these characteristics have worth (see, for example, Tomlinson, 1997). One such characteristic is self-regulation, usually taken to mean setting professional Standards *and* making judgements when it is alleged they are breached, through disciplinary action – processes thought to confer status and demonstrate trust.

Treating teachers as professionals means entrusting them with defining professional Standards in the public interest, at the point of entry and at significant milestones in the professional lives of teachers. It means doing so without fear of 'producer capture' or of the exclusivity and protectionism typified by some trade and professional guilds of the past. The constitution of the Council, which brings together teachers and the community of interest in teaching, provides a structural defence against producer capture. The Council will want and expect to play a more significant role in the review of other teaching Standards and the development of new professional Standards when appropriate and useful. With the advent of the GTC, the teaching profession 'polices' Standards it does not set. The Secretary of State for Education and Skills might take an early opportunity to address this anomaly.

References

Department for Education and Employment (DfEE) (1998) *Teaching: High Status, High Standards*. Circular 4/98. London: DfEE.

Department for Education and Skills (DfES) and Teacher Training Agency (TTA) Requirements for Initial Teacher Training. London: DfES/TTA.

Furlong, J. (2000) *Higher Education and the Professionalism of New Teachers*. London: CVCP/SCOP, drawing on Hirst, P. (1996) The demands of professional practice and preparation for teachers. In J. Furlong and R. Smith (eds.) *The Role of Higher Education in Initial Teacher Training.* London: Kogan Page.

General Teaching Council for England (GTCE) (2000) *Initial Advice on the Review of Circular 4/98*. London: GTCE.

GTCE (2001) *Professional Learning Framework*. London: GTCE.

GTCE (2002) *Professional Code for Teachers*. London: GTCE.

Ozga, J. (1997) in I. Menter *et al* (eds.) *Work and Identity in the Primary School: A Post-Fordist Analysis*. Buckingham: Open University Press.

Sayer, J. (2000) *The General Teaching Council*. London: Cassell.

Tomlinson, J. (1997) in H. Bines and J. Welton (eds.) *Managing Partnership in Teacher Training and Development*. London: Routledge.

Since 1992, partnership has been officially acknowledged to be an important feature of initial teacher training and education (ITTE). Schools have been encouraged, via appendices to government circulars (and thus by ITTE providers), to take a fuller involvement beyond simply facilitating placements. The extent to which this opportunity has been taken up has varied enormously. Some schools have embraced the new challenges and have incorporated ITTE into the fabric of their operation. Others have continued to treat students as they always did, providing them with no more than a classroom and a class of children. And, of course, there has been the complete spectrum in between. It should also be said that there is still a significant minority of schools that choose not to take students.

Partnership in the revised Standards and requirements

Until the publication of the revised Standards in January 2002 (DfES/TTA, 2002), the requirement for providers to work in partnership with schools was always included as an appendix to circulars. It is a mark of the growing importance attached to this aspect of ITTE that this requirement is now part of the main body of the Standards. The intention is clear: 'partnership' is to be seen as having equal status with 'entry requirements', 'training and assessment' and 'quality assurance'.

In keeping with the change in tone throughout the new Standards (from Circular 4/98 – DfEE, 1998), the language used to set out the expectations for management of the partnership is less peremptory. In the earlier document, three out of six statements (under 'Partnership requirements') have negative elements. For example:

> '3.1.4 where partnership schools fall short of the selection criteria set, providers must demonstrate that extra support will be provided to ensure that the training provided is of a high standard' (DfEE, 1998).

Indeed, it is difficult to reconcile the term 'partnership' with what was actually described. On one analysis, the higher education institutions (HEIs) were intended to operate a system in which they required schools to reach certain standards before they could be trusted with students. Clearly, this would, if followed by the HEIs, have led to a very unequal partnership. Far from celebrating the opportunity to work in partnership, the impression is given of mistrust and doubt about the ability of schools to contribute meaningfully to the training of student teachers. (The pamphlet *Partners in Training* (TTA, 1999), circulated to schools at the same time as the publication of Circular 4/98, had as its subtitle 'Is your school good enough to work with trainees?'.) Of course, quality assurance is appropriate and necessary. But so it is with every aspect of teacher training. The final appendix of 4/98 is devoted to this issue and addresses it thoroughly. The inclusion of QA requirements within the Partnership Appendix is, therefore, unnecessary and conveys a distinctly negative tone.

In the revised Standards and requirements, *Qualifying to Teach* (DfES/TTA, 2002), the language is much more positive. There are seven statements outlining what is expected of the providers, none of which expresses any doubt about the ability of schools to contribute to ITTE. Far from focusing on the standards to be reached by schools, the requirements are on the providers to attend to their own performance; if any doubt is implied about the capacity of institutions to deliver, it is the HEIs themselves who are targeted. They (the providers) **must** '*work in partnership with schools … set up partnership agreements … make sure the partnership works effectively.*' (ibid. p. 16). Naturally, the performance of schools in ITTE must come under proper scrutiny, but there is no suggestion, implicit or otherwise, that schools are more likely to fall short than any other aspect of ITTE. *The whole* of the partnership has to work effectively; *all the training* has to be co-ordinated and consistent. This leads to the question: who will be responsible for the monitoring?

It is at this point that one needs to pause and question what 'the partnership' will actually look like. Is the partnership simply a relationship between schools and the HEI that exists for the duration of student placements, or is it a steering group which oversees ITTE?

The first impression given by the title of this section in *Qualifying to Teach* ('Management of the ITTE Partnership') is of a body of people working together, a committee or steering group overseeing either school-based ITTE or ITTE as a whole (as provided by that HEI). However, it is ambiguous and the detail that follows conveys a somewhat different message (though the brief nature of the statements gives some room for interpretation). Regulation 3.1 sets out the purposes that the partnership will exist for. Regulation 3.2 describes what partnership agreements will need to contain. Regulation 3.3 does two things: it gives the responsibility for driving the partnership to the provider (**not** jointly to both sides of the partnership): '*All providers must* make sure the partnership works effectively*' (DfES/TTA, 2002, p. 16).

It also links the partnership with other aspects of ITTE which one could call services to the students. There is no indication that 'the partnership' is to be an entity, a body of professionals overseeing the partnership as a process. Indeed, the partnership seems to be a functional and very limited arrangement. This is unfortunate because it could give leeway to HEIs who are less enthusiastic about school involvement to limit their partnership plans to the aforesaid functional arrangements.

Partnership in the non-statutory guidance

Much of the rest of this chapter refers to the non-statutory guidance on partnership which effectively underpins the revised Standards and requirements. At the time of writing the final version of the handbook has not been published and the draft consultation version is being updated. Whatever the final outcome, it is argued that the draft version is worthy of consideration as it is a clear indication of thinking about the development of partnership at national level.

Although there is a clear distinction between the revised Standards and the non-statutory guidance (one is statutory, the other isn't), it can be assumed that the handbook (DfES/TTA, 2001) outlines how the Teacher Training Agency (TTA) would prefer the Standards to be achieved. Certainly, there should not be any contradictions. There is, therefore, much more to be optimistic about when one goes to the handbook. Here, it is clear the TTA does intend there to be a partnership committee steering the development of HEI/school partnerships:

> *'All partners should share responsibility for the effectiveness of the partnership as a whole...'*

> *'the partnership will need collectively to establish structures and procedures to monitor and review...'* (ibid., p. 129).

There then follows a list of all the elements that go to make up the entire ITTE course, not just the school-based aspect. Thus, it is the intention for schools to be involved in assessing what the HEI does, just as much as the HEI is to be a part of assessing the schools' performance (i.e. a genuine and equal partnership). To some extent, this is an acknowledgement of what has already begun to take place in existing partnerships. It is none the less welcome because it reinforces current practice and provides encouragement to partnerships which aren't as far along the process.

Though there are arguments for making some of this statutory (and so cajole sometimes reluctant HEIs into genuine partnerships), it is consistent with the TTA's desire to allow an evolutionary approach to this issue. By making a basic minimum statutory, but explicitly setting out how they would see partnerships working in the best of circumstances, they are allowing for localised variation, and also for definition to be worked out in practice.

This whole area requires sensitive handling from the TTA, from individual HEIs and even (or especially) at school level. Despite the fact that some may feel there is a moral obligation to participate in the training of the next generation of practitioners, schools are not obliged to accept students. As remarked above, many schools choose not to do so. The reasons why schools *do* choose to accept them are frequently detailed in government circulars and pamphlets. The fact that this is done at all may be an indication that it is not obvious.

The handbook mentions five benefits, only one of which can easily be linked to the school's usual functions (i.e. the opportunities for professional development of staff). Of the other four benefits mentioned in the handbook, one is the moral obligation to be involved in training (see above); the other three are concerned with the tenuous advantages of being linked with an HEI and other partnership schools. The effects on children's education are not mentioned.

Student placements – costs

This is an important omission. It does in fact go to the heart of the matter. Schools are concerned solely with the education of children. Everything else that goes on in a school is usually seen as a supporting structure to this central purpose. So that, if a school is asked to take on any initiative, it is, either consciously or otherwise, measured against this purpose – will it contribute to it or lead to it being compromised? It is this concern that leads to many schools refusing to accept students or, even when they do accept them, failing to engage with partnership as fully as their local HEI would wish them to.

The reasoning behind this is not hard to appreciate. In the first place, the quality of students cannot be guaranteed. The chances of being given a weak student may, for some schools, outweigh the possible benefits of getting a strong one. Secondly, whatever the quality of the student, there is bound to be some loss of continuity as the student takes over from the class teacher: either in the content of the teaching or in the style of delivery. Most people would agree that stability is an important ingredient in children's education. Furthermore, any effort that is directed towards supporting students is not being given to the children.

Today's context is also highly relevant – schools are stretched almost to breaking point trying to cope with the constant flood of initiatives emanating from the government and/or the Department for Education and Skills (DfES). The two major teaching unions (NASUWT and NUT) are currently conducting a campaign against excessive workload. The government itself sponsored an investigation into this aspect of teaching because it recognised the validity of the complaint.

It is stating the obvious to say that mentoring students is hard work. There is, for all class teachers who have students, the necessity of setting aside time to discuss all the aspects of the placement – planning, the children, the practice of the teacher and student, the nature of the school and its routines. For the school-based tutor, there is the need to speak regularly with students and class teachers, observations to conduct, with feedback afterwards, as well as weekly seminars and the paperwork to complete.

For schools who have not previously been involved with mentoring students themselves, it can be intimidating to contemplate taking on this role. Even if the balance of costs/benefits is thought to be on the side of accepting students in the longer term, it will be unlikely to be perceived or achieved in the short term. In the first place, there will be the necessary training of the school-based tutor. Then, if the job is to be done properly, there will be the planning and preparation within the school as a whole and for each of the class teachers who will be accepting students. These 'costs' will be compounded by the uncertainty associated with taking on anything new.

The response of parents to having their children taught by students can also have some weight in the equation. Parents rarely appreciate the value of having their children taught by students. The best that one can usually hope for is an acknowledgement that teachers have to train somewhere. Although this is a relatively minor issue (especially for schools that believe in the value of having student teachers), it can tip the balance for schools that are uncertain whether to embark on the partnership road.

Schools that have a significant number of children with behavioural problems may also be reluctant to accept students. At Claremont (my own school), we accept a large number of students each year. However, there are almost always a small number of classes where we don't place students, because we consider the children too difficult to handle. On the same principle that one doesn't deliberately put a child in a failing situation, we don't put students where we anticipate that they will be unable to cope. Similarly, the effect on the children is likely to be detrimental. Thus far, they may be having a relatively successful year. The achievement of this success is likely to have been the result of a delicate process of building a relationship with them. A student (or anyone new) could destroy this. Schools with all, or almost all, their classes like this may take a similar decision to us at Claremont.

As was hinted at earlier, there is an issue of confidence involved in the prospect of taking on students for the first time. Mainly, this is a question of belief in the capacity to do the job successfully. However, implicated in this is the uneasiness generated by having students and college staff in the school. Individual teachers will be aware that their own practice will be subject to some scrutiny. Of course, they can be assured that they will not be formally judged – it is the students who have to 'pass' – but unquestionably there is some element of challenge involved in being observed by students, explaining one's own practice and discussing deeper issues than are, perhaps, normally raised in the daily life of school. On a similar theme, in the review of Circular 4/98, it was mentioned that some schools found the prospect of being part of Office for Standards in Education (OFSTED) inspections of ITTE daunting. Once again, this is perfectly understandable: few schools have a positive attitude towards OFSTED and will be unwilling to be part of an inspection, even when it does not directly affect them.

As was stated earlier, a number of documents have rehearsed the advantages which are supposed to accrue from accepting students in school. Yet there is still a shortage of such schools. As has been outlined above, there is clearly another side to the argument. There are definite costs in accepting students and these need to be acknowledged if more schools are to be brought into partnership. It is, in the end, a cost/benefit analysis. What we at Claremont find difficult and what I have learned about the difficulties experienced by other schools are described above. Thus, anyone attempting to persuade a school to take on anything additional will need to address these issues – particularly the effects on children's learning and on workload.

Student placements – benefits

Although the handbook arguably does a poor job of making a case for accepting students (see above), it is in fact a good place to start if one is to delve deeper into this issue:

> *'Effective school-based training also helps trainees and those who work with them to recognise ITTE as the first stage of a career-long professional development process, and to see schools as learning communities in which teachers seek to develop themselves and their colleagues as well as their pupils'* (DfES/TTA, 2001, p. 128).

The key term here is 'learning communities'. If the vision of the school accords with this term, then accepting students follows on naturally. Not only is the school widening its 'intake', it is displaying the confidence to open itself up to the scrutiny associated with inviting other professionals in and to learn from others.

If the school is in the habit of reflecting on its practice, then it will be less likely to feel apprehensive about discussing its performance with others. Indeed, setting its philosophy and practice against the standards of other institutions (the local HEI or other partnership schools) will be a more rigorous test than internal reflection.

If the school genuinely wants the best for its pupils, it will recognise that a living curriculum must be constantly open to reappraisal and thus welcome the opportunity to experience the new ideas and approaches brought by students. Of course, as with all new initiatives, judgement will need to be exercised to ensure that the children's educational needs are not compromised.

If the school and its staff are serious about continuing professional development (about learning for the staff and the institution as a whole), then working with students will provide an ideal opportunity for all the staff involved in the exercise:

> *'Demonstrating and explaining teaching methods to trainees, watching them teach, coaching them in how to improve, helping them understand how to unlock each child's potential – all these help good teachers to analyse and improve their own practice and their professional skills'* (TTA, 1999).

School-based tutors will have greater scope through their training, and those who desire to take things further are likely to have the chance to be involved with the partnership at a more demanding level – selecting, assessing and teaching trainees in college. Furthermore, being involved with the HEI will give the school a direct link with a provider of professional development.

Many of these advantages are mentioned in previous documents but for their full force to be felt, they do, I believe, need to be linked expressly with the vision of a learning community. If a school sees itself as such, then it is only the logistics and practicalities of accepting students which can stand in the way of this step.

Management of student placements

The handbook identifies key characteristics of effective partnership practice:

- *Clear management structures*
- *Open lines of communication between the partners*
- *High expectations that are defined collaboratively and shared by all partners*
- *Partners who are empowered and are clear about their accountability*
- *A shared commitment to the importance of school-based training* (DfES/TTA, 2001, p. 128).

The reference is, of course, to the whole of the partnership, particularly to the provider who will have the responsibility of setting up partnership arrangements. However, it serves as a good model for how the partnership should be handled in schools; all one needs to do is assume that 'partners' refers to class teachers, students, the school-based mentor and the link tutor. The model then works perfectly. This may not be particularly illuminating – any enterprise will work more effectively if it is thoroughly planned.

In fact, it is probably true to say that many schools will ensure that the operation runs smoothly, with teachers briefed appropriately, students given the necessary information and supported throughout their placement. The correct number of observations will be conducted and professional critiques and reports will be written about the students. However, such planning is limited to the successful completion of the exercise as a student placement, and no more. In order for the school's involvement in ITTE to contribute to its development as a learning community, planning will need to take place at a higher level.

In fact, the exercise is less likely to be successful if it is not addressed at this level. Accepting students has the potential to severely disrupt the life of a school for the duration of the placement. If long-term plans are put on hold while students are in school, there is, at the very least, likely to be some frustration for those who have made those plans. If, on the other hand, the student placement is expected, planned for and built into long-term plans, it will be welcomed and the benefits will be maximised.

If all staff have shared the school's vision and the integral part that school-based training has in it, they are far more likely to feel positive about students. If they accept that the best way to realise the benefits of having students is to enable them to become the best students they can, then each staff member is more likely to put in the effort to achieve this.

The critical issue of finance

The argument is, however, not limited to being true to a school's own vision. The practical benefits of accepting students are rarely fully acknowledged. Schools are paid for mentoring students (approximately ten pounds a day) and theoretically this money could find its way to providing extra resources for the children's education. However, in the numerous inventories of the benefits of having students, financial profit is never included. In fact, the money received is simply insufficient to cover the cost of supply whilst the school-based tutor mentors the students. But this is not the last word to be said on the material benefits of having students in school.

To take an extreme example: a final-year student who is extremely competent and displays an appetite for the job, rather than limiting herself to the 75% minimum required, actually asks to teach the class full time for the second half of her placement. In fact, such a scenario is not that unusual. Most schools that accept students will have experienced something like this.

Of course, there will be a need to monitor the student's performance, but essentially the class teacher is now available for other things than teaching his or her class. This may be in the form of covering classes (due to sickness or attendance on courses) or contributing to monitoring and evaluation by, say, observing other classes him- or herself or releasing other teachers to do a similar task. There are of course many other possibilities. But the point is that, because the school has been lucky enough to have a strong student, a teacher is made available to do other things than teach his or her class. From the example quoted, it may seem I am acknowledging that this is likely to be a rare occurrence. In fact, apart from placements which require students to work only with groups, there will almost always be some opportunities to release teachers for either single sessions or whole days.

And here we return to the subject of management. If someone has a clear oversight of the placement, knows the strengths and weaknesses of the student, knows the needs of the school, both in the immediate term (teacher absence) and in the longer term of monitoring and evaluation requirements, then, without exploiting the students in any way, the availability of teachers can be utilised to its best effect. Furthermore, this is more likely to occur if the school has been doing a good job with the students – helping them to get the best out of themselves, challenging them but assisting them to meet those challenges. In my experience, almost all students will demonstrate an appetite for teaching if they are supported appropriately. Once again, the key element is management.

Conclusion

There is still some way to go before successful partnership is the norm in teacher training. The TTA is, I believe, taking the correct approach: allowing the shape of it to be defined in practice. What the revised Standards do is to elevate the importance of Partnership to equality with other elements of good ITTE practice.

There is not the clearest of guidance in the handbook – the concepts of partnership as a process and 'the' partnership as a regulating body are used interchangeably leading to some vagueness. However, it is certainly clear from the handbook that the TTA believe in the creation of a body comprising representatives from schools and the HEI with extensive powers to monitor the whole of ITTE provision.

The elements for a good supporting case for partnership are present in the handbook but not articulated as precisely as they could have been. The importance of the concept of learning communities is mentioned but not stressed nearly enough. It is, in fact, central, not just to the future of partnership arrangements but to education generally.

That successful schools are well managed schools is a truism and perhaps conveys very little. What effective management means in practice is certainly not delineated often enough. Once again, the handbook goes some way to remedying this in its list of the key characteristics of effective partnerships. When the concept of a vision of a learning community is linked with effective management, it becomes clearer that this management needs to begin with the school development plan.

It takes vision, commitment and confidence to make school-based ITTE work. No matter how glibly the benefits of accepting students are proclaimed, they are not achieved easily or cheaply. Only if the potential and actual costs of undertaking this exercise are fully acknowledged and answered will more schools come on board and, ultimately, embrace the concept.

References

Department for Education and Employment (DfEE) (1998) *Teaching: High Status, High Standards*. Circular 4/98. London: DfEE.

Department for Education and Skills (DfES) and the Teacher Training Agency (TTA) (2002), *Qualifying to Teach: Professional Standards for Qualified Teacher Status and Requirements for Initial Teacher Training*. London: DfES/TTA.

Teacher Training Agency (TTA) (1999) *Partners in Training*. London: TTA.

Ever since the James Callaghan speech of 1976, the issue of 'standards' in teacher education has been on the political agenda. It is significant that the Standards of Circular 4/98 (DfEE, 1998) and those of *Qualifying to Teach* (DfES/TTA, 2002) are the Secretary of State's standards, not overtly the standards owned by the profession itself: rather, they are monitored and administered by government quango: either the Teacher Training Agency (TTA) or the Office for Standards in Education (OFSTED). This has profound implications for the concept of quality. The position also has profound implications for providers as part of their daily lives and shapes the experience of students. Three key aspects of the concept of quality underpin this context: quality control, quality assurance and quality enhancement. Key questions to be asked of the new Standards and proposed OFSTED approach are: how far do they strike the right balance between the three aspects of quality? Do they give the right emphasis to quality enhancement? Do they provide an appropriate basis for supporting the process of continuous improvement and meet the future needs of the teaching profession?

Quality control

Quality control is exercised at national level: the TTA uses the results of OFSTED inspections to exercise control by means of (1) a process of accreditation; and (2) a direct link between OFSTED grades and the allocation of student numbers and finance. This use represents a significant limitation to traditional concepts of university autonomy and implies that the raising of standards is a matter of external control, in which the role of OFSTED in establishing an inspection methodology and grading system is crucial.

The notion of improvement by inspection is easily suborned into a demand for compliance to externally imposed criteria and their use. The recent exercise in consultation is probably one of the largest and most detailed exercises in consultation undertaken in order to counter the potential accusations of imposition and enable government to claim that the views of providers and other interested parties are taken fully into consideration by ministers. It is, however, to be noted that the outcome of consultations is mediated by the TTA and OFSTED with little direct involvement or representation by the teaching profession as a whole or teacher educators in particular.

Quality assurance

Quality assurance is the viewpoint that gives expression to the concept of accountability. To whom is teacher education accountable? The answer in the present approach is: to the public (i.e. the government), in terms of cost effectiveness and standards. There are, of course, others: notably the teaching profession; the student teachers; and the universities who validate academic awards and in most cases recommend Qualified Teacher Status (QTS) status. The role of the TTA and OFSTED currently reflect the government (public) as the purse-holder and the bureaucracy that follows as a consequence. The role of the others to whom teacher education is accountable raises further key questions. In terms of the profession, what is the role of the General Teaching Council for England (GTCE)? In terms of the universities it is notable that the role of OFSTED relates only to the Standards for QTS. Who monitors the quality of the academic awards? The Quality Assurance Agency (QAA) has not undertaken this role. The position of double account-ability to OFSTED and the QAA has, however, to date been avoided. Nevertheless, a significant gap arises in terms of the academic standards of university awards, which may be a concern to the teaching profession, not least from the viewpoint of the long-standing commitment to an all-graduate profession. More open access to the teaching profession may lower standards through the separation of academic awards and QTS. Even more fundamental is the issue of how academic and professional standards are related. Other professions, such as law, medicine and social services, have remained committed to the link, not only for reasons of status but also as a means of assuring professional standards of the highest quality. In terms of QTS alone, a recent OFSTED report (*The Graduate Teacher Programme* – OFSTED, 2002a) has been critical of some of the new routes into teaching. The current shortage of teachers itself produces a tension between more open access and the maintenance of standards. The role of classroom assistants and the distinctiveness of their work from that of qualified teachers raise so far unexplored issues of roles and standards. The issue of accountability to student teachers themselves is rarely discussed.

There may well be significant differences between the perceptions of what students think they need or are offered and what the government thinks they need or the univer-sities think they offer. The quality of student evaluation is a neglected area that might achieve greater importance in an increased role for evaluation at the point of delivery and the inclusion of data from this source in a new OFSTED strategy.

Quality enhancement

However, quality control and quality assurance are arguably of less importance than 'quality enhancement'. It is our conviction that high standards rest not on external control or accountability, but on the way providers create a culture of high quality and a determination to seek to raise standards wherever and whenever possible. This implies that much more is needed than compliance and acceptance of criteria following consul-tation. To achieve the proactive culture indicated requires a stronger sense of ownership and a greater scope for provider autonomy. The dominance of quality control and assurance inhibits the development of a culture of quality enhancement. The thrust of the former is towards retrospection (what has been achieved, tested by inspection and various forms of 'measurement' typified by league tables), while the thrust of the latter is to build upon achievement, to innovate, to be future orientated and to respond to the diversity of need as determined at a local or regional level. Quality enhancement arises in contexts of collegiality, diversity and partnership; it reflects processes of course development, staff development, scholarship and research in an open ethos of debate; and it operates within a framework of democratic systems in which all participants understand that professional and academic autonomy is worthy of respect. Quality enhancement is not incompatible with external frameworks. National comparisons and frameworks are necessary. Independent inspection, for example, can contribute, providing the framework is the result of genuine collaboration nationally and works to a methodology and agenda undertaken in genuine partnership with the providers of teacher education. Collective responsibility for standards is fundamental.

Issues of collective responsibility

Consultation papers have been presented to everyone involved in initial teacher training and education (ITTE) at a largely technical level, built on unstated assumptions and modifying existing practice. Indeed, one of the frustrations of respondents to such consultation papers is the seeming straitjacket into which questions for response are placed and the lack of opportunity to challenge implicit assumptions that underpin practice. Indeed, the notions of reliability, validity, transparency and consistency of inspection methodology have seldom received detailed scrutiny, but are all fundamental to confidence in the system and all relate to the key concepts of quality and standards on which any satisfactory methodology can be constructed.

A culture of standardised, uniform compliance is not sufficient to motivate nor bring about the enhancement of standards; only honesty in identifying weaknesses, the endorsement of strengths and priorities, the encouragement of innovation and a strong focus on strategies for provider development will in the long run be effective. A system which gives priority to policing externally imposed regulations and in its operation penalises providers for apparent weaknesses is unlikely to inspire the necessary confidence to achieve shared goals. A recent National Primary Teacher Education Conference (NaPTEC) survey conducted independently by the Electoral Reform Services (February 2001) indicated a significant number of providers (69.1% of respondents) considered they had been inspected on the basis of a 'deficit' model of provision and standards. A key test of new OFSTED procedures in relation to the new Standards is whether or not they support ITTE and are likely to result in a significant change of perception by providers.

Ralph Tabberer, the Chief Executive of the TTA, has said publicly on more than one occasion that standards have risen significantly in teacher education and the Chief Inspector of Schools has recognised that providers have made a significant contribution to improving the quality of newly qualified teachers in our schools. Now is the time to build upon these positive indicators of change. It is clear that in the recent past, OFSTED has never engaged in a public way in a debate about the purpose, nature and role of OFSTED in raising standards in teacher education. There is no OFSTED mission statement.

Standards and Inspection

The link between standards and inspection is fundamental. An inspection methodology, however good, is pointless if misdirected. Standards and Inspection have to be responsive to the purposes of education as reflected in our culture and society and this is the core of any understanding of the validity of inspection.

It is a truism that society is facing change at an unprecedented rate and that education as a consequence must expect rapid change. Any set of standards should, therefore, on the one hand, not be set in stone and will, on the other, expect to be rigorous and set new challenges. A system of inspection must be responsive to this context. Given that change may be for better or worse, it is fundamental that the underlying values that nform the system are identified. The statement of values presented in the Standards is, therefore, to be warmly welcomed. However, like all value statements they are subject to differences of interpretation, differences of priority and differences of application. Hence, they 'give rise' to degrees of ambiguity, controversy and contextual difference. As such they are not readily measurable and present a challenge to any system of inspection, which is expected to assess compliance by providers. Recognition of contextual diversity and the notions of comparability as distinct from uniformity are essential in approaching the issues. While providers can be expected to meet the Standards expressed as values, they need to do so in an autonomous way that meets the needs of schools both nationally and in local/regional contexts. The mission statement of a provider and the ways in which the values expressed in the mission are implemented in the light of their circumstances and needs should to be taken into account by OFSTED. Moreover, the ways in which a provider holds itself internally accountable and seeks to give 'expression' to its mission are fundamental. Self-evaluation and the related strategies for self-development are integral elements of reaching clearly articulated standards of achievement. The approach of OFSTED needs to be as sensitive to the context of the provider as it is to the demands of the government or the TTA.

Validity and some implications

The issue of 'values' is, however, not the only aspect of the Standards that gives rise to questions of validity. In its response to the TTA/OFSTED consultation, NaPTEC drew attention to a major weakness in the Standards, in particular the absence of any explicit model(s) of teaching and learning in relation to the primary curriculum and little importance attached to such key concepts as creativity and problem-solving. The lack of emphasis upon a critical, analytical understanding of teaching and learning, or support for flexible, creative approaches to learning places in question how far the Standards give expression to the intellectual (therefore academic) basis of teaching, or the needs of the student teacher and his or her acquisition of a sound basis for future professional development. The lack of a coherent rationale for ITTE, induction and continuous professional development is a serious weakness in itself, but is exacerbated by the dominance of quality control and assurance perspectives. Of course the models of learning and teaching that are available reflect a variety of perspectives and any one may be open to ambiguity and/or variety of interpretation. Control has been especially evident in relation to the areas of literacy and numeracy and it is important that the distinction between the Standards and the non-statutory guidance is maintained; but generalised standards themselves are insufficient unless contextualised within strategies adopted by providers. The need to take account of such strategies, the providers' priorities, their basis in experience, research evidence, scholarship and the perception of stakeholders (e.g. students, headteachers) are all-important considerations. Inspection based on outcomes does not of itself lead to improvement; only the development of provision prior to inspection and the action following the analytical reporting of inspection together lead to improvement. An inspection methodology of a more broadly based kind is necessary in order to produce reports of a quality and effectiveness that fulfil these functions.

The purposes of inspection

The main aims or purposes of inspection were first formulated by the TTA and OFSTED in July 1996 and repeated with minor revisions in 1998, on this occasion adding a reference to ensuring consistency of Standards. In each case, emphasis is on the outcomes of training (i.e. how well teachers 'perform as teachers' at the end of their courses and their first year as newly qualified teachers). The wording in the aims expressed in the 2001 consultation is broadly consistent with the earlier statements but key words and phrases such as 'public accountability', 'compliance' and the 'statutory link between funding and quality' are now prominent while references to features of quality enhancement (e.g. providers own strategy for improvement and self-evaluation) appear in a separate paragraph. Features of quality enhancement could fairly be said to receive greater emphasis in 2001, but they appear in a subordinate role to the main aim of quality assurance. There is no discussion of any principled relationship and 'continuous improvement' is featured in the paragraph devoted to quality assurance. Indeed, the single-minded emphasis on outcomes at a prescribed point in an individual's professional development and the emphasis on 'performance' risk a superficial approach which neglects the links between contexts, goals, processes and outcomes in the education of a teacher, and points to the need for inspection methodology to enhance the role of self-evaluation by providers.

Even at the level of outcomes, the past practice of inspection has suffered from a major weakness. If inspection of outcomes is to go beyond identifying a threshold, the issues of commonly shared and understood criteria are fundamental in order to achieve reliable assessment. Provision of such agreed criteria by OFSTED is essential but none have been proposed. Small samples of observation of teaching by inspectors exacerbate the problem. Moreover, while many providers have produced their own such criteria, there is no certainty that they match the assumptions of particular inspectors or cover the eventuality of two parties disagreeing on the criteria to be applied. Moreover, interpretation of such criteria depends upon prior assumptions, priorities and contextual application. Once again the appropriate link between a central framework and consistency and rigour of a provider's approach and interpretation is of critical importance.

A particular tension arises in this context. On the one hand, professional integrity on the part of providers is essential and a soundly based system of provider evaluation is to be expected. The dangers of rationalising self-interest or a damaging defensiveness are to be recognised. These dangers may arise not so much from inspection itself but from the uses to which the outcomes of inspection are put (e.g. the TTA allocations process). Within the inspection process itself an agreed framework and methodology for inspection could provide the necessary framework. A collaborative approach would match the concept of collective responsibility. It has been common practice for QAA reviews to make use of the role of facilitator in visits and the review is based on peer judgements. While QAA approaches may themselves have weaknesses, these principles have validity in an approach based on these two principles. A framework and methodology should be jointly agreed and a system of inspection using both independent OFSTED inspectors and a provider peer group would appear to be a constructive way forward, albeit unlikely to be achievable within current timescales for implementing a new approach.

The proposed framework

The earlier framework (the 1996 and 1998 versions) was based on a structure of areas for inspection known as cells and reflected a period before the current range of new routes into teaching had been designed and introduced. As such, it has not been clear how far the existing framework has remained appropriate. The tensions of widening access and maintaining standards must be addressed. The principle expressed in the consultation papers that the Standards should apply to *all* routes into teacher education is to be welcomed. The issue then arises as to how OFSTED will inspect the variety of routes in order to provide the required quality assurance.

Rather than a straitjacket of uniformity, OFSTED are seeking an approach that offers more differentiation. It is clear that differences between primary and secondary approaches have always been necessary in practice. However, the increasing range of routes that can be offered by large providers prompts consideration of a more radical approach (i.e. a quality audit of a whole of a provider's range of ITTE activities). Following the QAA and other models, audit is the process by which self-evaluation is checked for validity and reliability. Where weaknesses are identified in the audit, a more in-depth review of particular areas or issues would be undertaken. Collaborative teams would undertake such an audit. The present proposals do not go as far as to propose a system of audit and follow-up, but could perhaps be seen as offering significant steps in this direction. An audit model would parallel the likely future direction of the QAA. The key OFSTED proposal is that '*Where there are several routes to QTS within the same provision, all the routes on offer should be covered by the inspection and grades awarded for the overall provision*' (OFSTED/TTA, 2001). This offers a more holistic approach to inspection but raises key issues to do with sampling, comparability and equivalence of approach and the relative balance of judgements between routes which need to be taken into account when reaching judgements and arriving at grades. Both audit and the OFSTED proposals would lighten the potential burden of inspections but the issues of reliability need to be addressed. The longer intervals between full inspections (of whatever kind) are to be welcomed if the associated key elements of providers' quality enhancement strategies are to be given the space and opportunity to take effect. However, the effectiveness of the proposals relates to how their use for the allocation process is applied. It is our view that while quality control requires non-compliant providers to be denied accreditation, the present method for allocation of numbers and/or finance has an effect that is punitive rather than serving developments offering quality enhancement.

The current OFSTED proposals (OFSTED/TTA, 2001) make some progress in raising the profile of providers' self-evaluation and the expectation that providers will construct improvement plans. OFSTED propose that '*Short inspections should focus on management and quality assurance, include provider's self-evaluations and improvement plans and be supplemented by subject specific evidence supplied by a specialist inspector*' (ibid.). This proposal places management and quality enhancement issues in a position of lower priority than quality assurance and control, since the long inspections appear to remain in many key aspects unchanged in character. This position reverses our view of a long inspection based on audit and self-evaluation of providers and shorter inspections arising therefrom. Shorter inspections on our model would either follow up issues arising from the audit and/or monitor progress (e.g. in relation to action plans). The OFSTED proposal refers to short inspections involving subject specialist inspectors. This may or may not be necessary depending on the nature of the issues involved and may follow from the model of the primary curriculum (based on traditional subjects) presented in the Standards. This model itself raises questions regarding the reliability of OFSTED judgement in situations where only partial evidence is available to inspectors.

Nevertheless, the steps towards more holistic inspection proposed are not the only positive features of the new proposals. The structure of the 1996 and 1998 frameworks were based upon a nine-cell framework. However, the new proposal suggests a three-cell structure: training quality (T); Standards achieved by trainees (S) and management and quality assurance (M). Two questions arise: is the reduction in the number of cells appropriate? And what is the relationship and balance of priorities between them? The reduction in the number of cells avoids partial overlap, confusion over the correct location of evidence and minimises the risk of cumulative punishment for weaknesses identified more than once. However, the relative importance of each cell is enhanced. Some of the nine cells were previously not directly inspected, in particular those related to management and quality assurance. The new proposals indicate that this will change, although the relative weighting of the three cells in the Standards, the training of mentors, mentoring itself and evaluation all involve time and substantial costs. Schools already consider the task underfunded and both schools and higher education partners consider they are subsidising partnerships. Moreover, primary schools in particular consider that they are not given the staffing to permit the necessary time for non-teaching responsibilities such as partnership involvement and mentoring, in particular, to be properly undertaken. Both the methods and scale of funding need fundamental review. This should include provision for school-based partners, alongside other partners, being involved with OFSTED in the independent process of inspection (see earlier comments). Such problems pose major issues for OFSTED inspection whether in terms of methodology (e.g. principles of sampling or a reliable methodology) or the validity of outcomes. Collaborative, urgent and extensive dialogue between OFSTED and providers is necessary if these issues are to be overcome, let alone action by the government on matters of funding.

Inspection and grading

Finally, the difficulties of grading and the purposes to which grading are put raise fundamental issues with regard to OFSTED inspection. The difficulties arising from the inspection of the M cell are likely to be exacerbated by grading and allocations. More fundamentally, grading and allocations methodologies build upon questionable priorities. The current proposals reflect the priorities of quality control and assurance rather than quality enhancement. Moreover, grading and allocations have a symbiotic relationship that expresses the dominance of a policing approach and produces instability and uncertainty in the resourcing of providers. The proposed four-point grading system is closely related to allocations systems that distinguish not only between those who are

non-compliant and others, but also distinctions between very good, satisfactory, unsatisfactory and non-compliant. The allocations system penalises providers other than those
judged to be very good, seeking to redistribute numbers towards the best or better
providers. The importance or grading of the new M cell are not clear. Previous practice
and the link between the M cell and short inspections may indicate a lower priority for
the M cell than the S and T cells. This would reflect directly an emphasis on the quality of
training outcomes.

Nevertheless, the new direct inspection of the M cell indicates enhanced emphasis on
this area and needs consideration in the light of the new standards and the expectations
presented in the light of any non-statutory guidance. The new Standards require
providers to *prepare and support all staff involved in training* and *make sure that the
partnerships work effectively*, referring to co-ordination, consistency and continuity
across the various contexts in which it takes place. These requirements are at the least
very demanding and at the worst unmanageable. The quality assurance requirements
lend further significance to this area and raise the issue of whether present provision
inspected against these requirements is likely to produce valid and reliable judgements.
Clearly the methods and scope of providers' self-evaluation are a key element. However,
the issues go far deeper and relate to two problems already known to the TTA: whether
there are sufficient schools in partnership with higher education and the quality of the
schools that already participate. A further problem is the high turnover of participating
schools from year to year. The training of mentors in schools and the scope and scale of
school involvement in partnership are also matters of concern. The lack of a clear agreed
approach to criteria for assessing teaching competence exacerbates these concerns.
Ensuring quality across large numbers of diverse schools, for example over 1,000 in some
large providers, is particularly challenging. Moreover, the requirement that providers
meet students' 'individual' needs raises the stakes even higher depending on the level of
expectation involved. This, of course, may vary from one route to QTS to another. The
difficulties arising in the Graduate Teacher Programme point to particular problems in
the more limited provision.

In order to meet high standards, it needs to be recognised that quality costs! However, a
useful distinction can be drawn between unsatisfactory providers and non-compliance.
It would seem more problematic to distinguish between 'very good' and 'satisfactory'. A
three-grade system (Satisfactory, Unsatisfactory, Non-compliant) would permit OFSTED
inspection to focus much more clearly on quality enhancement and avoid the pitfalls of
providers being penalised for factors beyond their control which adversely affect grades.
While we recognise that quality should relate to funding, serious consideration should
be given to a major change to the concept and methodology of allocations. The recent
OFSTED report on their consultations indicated that providers have wider concerns about
allocations that go well beyond the technical links between OFSTED gradings and TTA
allocations. A more constructive and creative relationship between OFSTED and
providers would follow, together with a greater willingness to manage the risks involved
in creating more open access to potential teachers. This would release time and energy
for the support of trainees, improve retention rates, release resources and raise
confidence in developing routes that meet more directly the diverse needs of trainees
and the future needs of the teaching profession.

Conclusion

In conclusion, it could be said that OFSTED shows an increasing commitment to quality enhancement while being obliged to operate a system dominated by concerns for quality control and assurance. Until political opinion supports a shift in priorities and a different allocations system is devised, providers are likely to find one unmanageable system replaced by another unmanageable system.

References

Department for Education and Employment (DfEE) (1998) *Teaching: High Status, High Standards*. Circular 4/98. London: DfEE.

Department for Education and Skills (DfES) and Teacher Training Agency (TTA) (2002) *Qualifying to Teach: Professional Standards for Qualified Teacher Status and Requirements for Initial Teacher Training*. London: DfES/TTA.

Office for Standards in Education (OFSTED) (1996) *Framework for the Assessment of Quality and Standards in Initial Teacher Training*. London: OFSTED.

OFSTED (1998) *Framework for the Assessment of Quality and Standards in Initial Teacher Training*. London: OFSTED.

OFSTED (2002a) *The Graduate Teacher Programme*. MM 1346. London: OFSTED.

OFSTED (2002b) *Inspection Arrangements for Initial Teacher Training 2002/3 Onwards: Report on the Consultation*. HMI 378. London: OFSTED.

Office for Standards in Education (OFSTED) and Teacher Training Agency TTA (2001) *Inspection: Arrangements for Initial Teacher Training 2002/3 Onwards*. London: OFSTED/TTA.

Teacher Training Agency (TTA) (2001) *Standards for the award of Qualified Teacher Status and Requirements for Initial Teacher Training. Consultation Document*. London: TTA.

Chapter 4: The challenge of inclusion in developing initial teacher training and education programmes
Andrew Waterson

Introduction

'Far from developing a "classless" society, the English educational system is still prey, in the twenty-first century, to ... being organised along lines of social class. Historically, the working classes have constantly been "found out" in education; discovered to be inferior, less cultured, less clever than the middle classes ... Both finding and losing yourself are about a lack in relation to the academic. A lack originally identified and hollowed out in the bourgeois imaginary and then fixed in the working classes ... most of all the lack lies in our political elites: those policy makers who fail to care, cynically dissemble and refuse to recognise the connections between educational and wider social contexts. However, I would also like to suggest that that lack lies closer to home – in our lack of care, lack of political will. At the beginning of the twenty-first century we still do not have a valued place within education for the working classes and for that we, the middle classes, must all collectively be held responsible' (Reay, 2001, pp. 343–44).

Social inclusion has become a major political, social and educational agenda at the turn of the millennium and it is to be expected therefore that it would figure more prominently in any prescription for initial teacher education (ITE). But the stage is essentially problematic as so many of the concepts are competing, fragmentary and elusive. At the outset a major concern must be that initial teacher *training* cannot hope to address issues concerned with values and attitudes for, as Stenhouse (1975, p. 80) indicates:

'training ... is concerned with the acquisition of skills and successful training results in capacity in performance ...'

The two Teacher Training Agency (TTA) circulars outlining the Standards for ITE in the 1990s (Circulars 14/93 and 4/98) both focused heavily on the training in competencies and therefore capacity in performance. The new 2002 Standards seek to make a move towards a more holistic approach with the introduction of a section on professional values and practice as well as several aspects of inclusion. If these professional values are to be realised in practice there will need to be a move towards *'the notion of the reflective, self-critical, analytical professional'* (TTA, 2001a, p. 8). Reflective practitioners will need the experience of initial teacher *education* and this should be much more concerned with *initiation* and *induction.* Initiation is concerned with familiarisation with social values and norms and induction is concerned with the introduction into 'thought' systems of a culture (Stenhouse, 1975). If these professional values are to be reality and not just rhetoric they need to have a major impact on how teachers are to be trained in the future and this will be discussed in more detail at the end of this chapter.

It's not only the issue of initial teacher training versus education that requires clarification: it is also the whole issue of inclusion itself that requires clarification and this will be dealt with in detail in the following section. But by way of introduction it is important to recognise that the move towards inclusion implies that some have been and are currently being excluded. Schools are being required (OFSTED, 2000; DfEE/QCA, 1999) to become more inclusive across a range of areas where previously children have been in some sense excluded: disability, special educational needs (SEN), gender, ethnicity, English as an additional language, as well as social class have all been areas where children have not always received equality of opportunity within the English education system. Gillborn and Mirza (2000) have described the outcomes of these inequalities and they make compelling reading. They found that the inequalities associated with ethnic origin and particularly social class background are considerably larger than those associated with gender. More worryingly, whilst there has been an overall improvement in the standards achieved by all pupils in the past ten years, the gap between the most and the least successful is growing: whilst the performance of children from Indian and white, non-manual backgrounds at GCSE has improved significantly, that of the children of Afro-Caribbean, Bangladeshi and Pakistani pupils has improved only slightly. Comparisons of pupils from similar class backgrounds show marked inequalities of attainment across different ethnic groups.

As the government white paper, *Excellence in School* (DfEE, 1997a p.10), put it :

> *'The problem with our education system has been that excellence at the top is not matched by high standards for all children. Too many pupils still fail to achieve what they can. Too many leave school with few or no qualifications. And there are unacceptable differences between different groups of pupils and between schools. This cannot be allowed to continue. We want success for everyone.'*

Inclusion, educational or social? The bombardment of schools with initiatives

The term inclusion, as with many terms applied currently in educational contexts, is a disputed concept. Each group of educationists and politicians concerned with a particular aspect of education has claimed it as their own. This results in a term which is fragmented, elusive and entirely problematic resulting in difficulties in gaining agreement of definition.

Weiner (2001) indicates the ideologically driven nature of social inclusion in the way that it addresses not just the gradations of inequality but the forces and mechanisms within society that affect it. Central to *social* inclusion are the ideas of social justice and the role of citizenship within a social democracy in terms of equality, responsibilities and rights. The outcome of this is that the proponents of inclusion believe that all children whatever their ability have a right to learn together and that there are no reasons for keeping them separate (CSIE, 2002). Critics (Wilson, 1999) point out the innate logical contradiction of all pupils being appropriately competent to be *educationally* included in activities citing as examples the learning of quadratic equations and playing in an orchestra. What Wilson (ibid.) does concede is the ideological reminder that schools should not write off children who are less gifted in particular areas of learning but address the question of what learning activities are best suited to what pupils. This again highlights the importance of the values and the concomitant processes within the educational institution.

There appear to be three distinctive but overlapping areas of activity in inclusion: children with disabilities and SEN; children in danger of being excluded (suspended) from school; and children who, due to the schools' and/or the teachers' attitudes and values towards particular groups, are to a greater or lesser extent not fully included in the curriculum and life of the school. These groups might include gender, social class, ethnic origin, travellers' children, refugees and 'cared-for' children.

Inclusion in terms of children with SEN and/or disability

The proponents of this area of inclusion promote the *integration* of children in mainstream schools instead of being excluded in special schools and their *inclusion* in both the school as a community and the curriculum itself (Ainscow, 1997). Much of this is supported by international agreements and legislation. The Salamanca Statement (UNESCO, 1994 p.ix) calls upon governments to '*adopt as a matter of law or policy the principle of inclusive education, enrolling all children in regular schools unless there are compelling reasons for doing otherwise*'. The provision, normally, for the education of all children in mainstream schools became statutory under the Education Act 1996. The new Labour government then set out its agenda in a Green Paper (DfEE, 1997b, p. 43) which indicated:

> '*The ultimate purpose of special educational needs provision is to enable young chil-dren to flourish in adult life. There are, therefore, strong educational, as well as social and moral, grounds for educating children with their peers. We aim to increase the level and quality of inclusion in mainstream schools*' (DfEE, 1997b, p.43).

The Special Educational Needs and Disability Act 2001 set out the requirements in relation to disability equality that schools must meet; these include from September 2002 the duty to:

- not treat disabled pupils less favourably;
- take reasonable steps to ensure that disabled pupils are not disadvantaged; and
- improve the physical environment and written communication so as to increase disabled pupils' participation.

There are now two codes of practice – one for disability (DRC, 2002) and one for SEN (DfES, 2001) – which indicate how schools might be expected to become compliant with the legal requirements. However, this is also an area for debate: is inclusion the most effective strategy for children with SEN? As Hornby (1999) indicates, there is a lack of research evidence to support this and he advocates the adoption of less idealistic policies regarding the inclusion of children with SEN in mainstream settings.

Inclusion as opposed to exclusion from school

Increasing numbers of children are being excluded from schools; between 1990 and 1996 there was a four-fold increase in the rate of exclusions nationally (Hallam and Castle,

2001). This overlaps with minority ethnic group issues in that Afro-Caribbean pupils are up to six times more likely to be excluded than white British children and the research outlines the damaging impact this can have on this group's academic progress (Runnymede Trust, 1998). The government has sought to address the issue of pupil exclusions in its Circular 10/99: *Social Inclusion: Pupil Support* (DfEE, 1999). This aims to reduce the risk of disaffection among pupils by supporting the development of schools' pastoral and disciplinary policies. The good practice promoted in the circular is widely quoted and supported elsewhere (e.g. Parson, 1999; Gillborn and Mirza, 2000; Hallam and Castle, 2001). The 'good principles' which schools are encouraged to draw on include:

- setting good habits early;
- early intervention;
- rewarding achievements;
- supporting behaviour management;
- working with parents;
- involving pupils;
- commitment to equal opportunities;
- identifying underlying causes; and
- study support (adapted from DfEE, 1999, Chap. 2).

Guidance is also given on how to handle signs of disaffection, the use of exclusion and strategies for the re-integration of excluded pupils.

Social inclusion: internal exclusion and the expectancy effect

Rogers (1982) examines the process whereby teachers' expectations of pupils are subtly communicated, taken in and acted out by the pupils themselves; it is an uncomfortably persuasive argument as much of it accords with the experience of working with 'at-risk' groups of children. As a statistician once told me, one of the most significant predictors of success in the educational system is the child's first name; not too many Waynes and Kylies do that well. Even where pupils from 'at risk' groups are present in schools they are often not fully included and, as was discussed in the introduction to this chapter, are thereby disadvantaged in terms of their achievements. For example, the attainments of Afro-Caribbean pupils become progressively lower, in comparison to the overall attainment of pupils, as they progress through the educational system. This is often attributed to their alienation from school. However, as Gillborn and Mirza (2000, p. 17) found:

'Research evidence, however, challenges such stereotypes about alienation, disenchantment, and lack of motivation. In comparison with white peers of the same sex and social class background, for example, studies show that Black pupils tend to display higher levels of motivation and commitment to education. This has been documented in relation to pupils' enthusiasm for school, rates of attendance and support for homework. It is also clearly indicated in the relatively greater encouragement to pursue further education that African-Caribbean pupils receive from their families and in the young people's decisions to pursue such study, often despite negative experiences in the compulsory system. A good deal of qualitative research, for example, argues that

Black pupils are often treated more harshly (in disciplinary terms) and viewed with low-er teacher expectations on the basis of teachers' assumptions about their motivation and ability. Research evidence also suggests that more attention should focus on the processes by which schools identify "ability" and plan to ensure that pupils from differ-ent ethnic and social class backgrounds make the most of their potential.'

The 'at-risk' groups come from a wide spectrum of the community, including gender, social class, minority ethnic groups, travellers, refugees, speakers of English as an additional language, young carers (of a sick or disabled person), children in the care of local authorities, families under stress and pregnant schoolgirls and teenage mothers DfEE, 1999; OFSTED, 2001). This adds to the complexity of meeting their needs (and, by implication, the initial education of teachers).

Similarly the historical and legislative background is equally complex. For example, after the publication of the report of the Stephen Lawrence inquiry (Macpherson, 1999), the Government published the Race Relations Amendment Act 2000 which placed a series of new requirements on public bodies (including schools) under the general duty of promoting racial equality'. The Commission for Racial Equality (CRE) provided schools with guidance on how to audit their provision (CRE, 2000) and more recently have published a code of practice (currently in draft) with which schools are to be compliant by 31 May. The code outlines three general duties and four specific duties, which are to:

General duties:
- Eliminate unlawful racial discrimination.
- Promote equality of opportunity.
- Promote good relations between people of different racial groups.

Specific duties:
- Prepare and maintain a written race equality policy.
- Assess the impact of policies.
- Monitor the impact of policies.
- Observe the employment duties.

The TTA has also set out guidance for providers of ITE (TTA, 2000) which attempts to provide practical details on how to prepare student teachers to implement support in schools as well as the recruitment, retention and support of minority ethnic trainee teachers.

What impact does this have on classroom practice?

The purpose of answering this question is to assess the impact that inclusion *ought* to have on ITE. It is not simply a question of understanding and conveying to students *what* inclusion is but, more importantly, how it is to be implemented in practice.

The National Curriculum (DfEE/QCA, 1999) now places statutory obligations on schools in terms of inclusion at the beginning of the Programmes of Study. It sets out and discusses three principles for inclusion. This is a new departure in that previous versions have focused only on *what* was to be taught and not on *how* it was to be taught. The preamble indicates that

> 'In planning and teaching the National Curriculum, teachers are to have due regard t the following principles' (DfEE/QCA 1999, p.30).

This has major implications for both schools and ITE. The three principles are now a statutory requirement and teachers must therefore be trained to plan and teach on the basis of these. The principles are:

1. setting suitable learning challenges;
2. responding to pupils' diverse learning needs – creating effective learning environment securing motivation and concentration, providing equality of opportunity, using appro priate assessment approaches and setting targets for learning; and
3. overcoming potential barriers to learning and assessment for individuals and groups c pupils – pupils with SEN, disabilities or English as an additional language.

Similarly, the Office for Standards in Education (OFSTED), in their guidance to school inspectors, attempts to bring the various strands associated with inclusion together so that they are manageable (OSTED, 2001). They raise three questions which inspectors are to answer through focusing on significant groups who may not be deriving sufficient benefit from their education.

1. Do all pupils get a fair deal at school?
2. How well does the school recognise and overcome barriers to learning?
3. Do the school's values embrace inclusion and does its practice promote it?

At the time of writing schools are being faced with becoming compliant with three new codes of practice. In terms of SEN, the categorisation of learning difficulties has been replaced by a much greater focus on the identification and meeting of children's needs and the five-stage approach by 'School Action' and 'School Action Plus'. In relation to disability and race equality, schools must implement the requirements listed above. This will mean they will need to audit, review and revise their provision and practices in these areas. If the lack of inclusion within the educational system is to be addressed, this will need to have significant impact on schools' approaches to teaching and learning, the nature and content of the curriculum, how pupils are assessed, how their progress is monitored by social and educational grouping, and how the relationships within the school and with the community it serves are conducted. Student teachers will need to be educated for very different educational settings.

Many ITE providers may well feel they have been addressing these principles and practices for many years through their courses. What is equally apparent is that it is the same teachers that ITE providers trained and are currently working in schools that are responsible for the lack of social and educational inclusion and the manifest disaffection and inequalities in attainments between different groups. The only implication from this is that ITE programmes also require radical change.

The impact of inclusion on initial teacher education

How are ITE providers to approach the new demands of educational inclusion? First, it is necessary to look to the student teachers themselves. If central to the issue of inclusion is the concern for equality of opportunity and social justice then the attitudes, values and ideas – the ideological perspective students bring with them is of prime importance. It is not my view that we should only recruit those student teachers who aspire to some social reconstructivist perspective; that would be the antithesis of social democracy, would stifle debate and make student seminars sterile. But we do need to recruit students who have a propensity for critical reflection and academic debate and who are looking to develop and refine through experience not just their competence as a teacher but a practical understanding of the issues that underpin what they do. Schon's (1983) view of reflection on and in action should be central. Inclusive education is much more than a matter of competencies and standards. In the same way that ITE providers often conduct their own assessments of literacy, should we now be focusing on prospective students' propensity for critical self-reflection and looking at ways of assessing this robustly?

Secondly, of course, we need to consider the teaching and the model of inclusive practice that teacher education institutions provide. There is the issue of the ability of ITE providers to include differing groups within their programmes. Their record here is not entirely noteworthy. For example, teaching has failed to recruit proportionately from minority ethnic groups who are significantly under-represented within the profession. Recent research (Carrington et al., 2001) into the views and experiences of student teachers and newly qualified teachers from ethnic minorities showed they had made the commitment to become teachers often at considerable personal cost. They were highly motivated and committed to teaching frequently with altruistic motives such as the importance of themselves as role models within their own communities and the significant part they can play in all-white schools. The intrinsic satisfaction of teaching was also highly rated. Many ethnic minority students were older than their white peers and, in consequence, faced financial hardship. Training grants and salaries will need to support these students between careers. Several students were anxious about the experience of racial harassment and how they might be treated in mainly white schools although, in practice, these concerns were largely unfounded. Nevertheless, partnerships between ITE providers and schools will from 31 May 2002 be required by law to ensure that procedures are in place to tackle racial harassment (and other forms of discrimination) and that students are suitably reassured that this will be taken seriously. Recruitment remains a central issue – no student wants to feel they are being more favourably treated and that they have been included on any grounds other than merit. But some of the administrative procedures present obstacles, especially for overseas students, and these need to be streamlined. The impression created by the Postgraduate Certificate in Edcuation (PGCE) staff in the selection process seems critical. As Jones (1999, p. 152) puts it:

'The small number of role models from ethnic minority groups desperately needs to be rectified and although teaching remains an understandably low career priority for some, those who do want to accept the challenge of teaching should not have to fight their way past layers of institutionalised racist practices.'

Thirdly, the curriculum student teachers' experience needs to be reviewed. There are two commonly proposed approaches to dealing with issues of equality of opportunity – permeation and discrete elements. Permeation models alone have largely been found to be ineffective (ibid.) and there will need to be both a direct and integrated approach to inclusion. This will need to involve dedicated sessions where issues of both personal and professional ideology are raised and examined as well as the issues and effective practices that will promote social and educational inclusion. These principles and practices must then underpin and permeate ITE programmes: this again needs to have a twofold impact on both the content and context of our programmes. Central to all this will be the role of partnership schools in grounding these understandings in professional practice; any model of inclusion within ITE must be predicated on meeting the needs of individual students and much of this is likely to be dependent on the quality of education they receive in schools.

What then, in practice, will the ITE curriculum need to address? If we are to model 'good practice' then OFSTED (2000) provides one of the more comprehensive frameworks. OFSTED indicates that educational institutions will need to carry out the following (as shown in italics):

- *Monitor learner performance and the standards achieved by different groups*: this will mean that students teachers will need to be trained how to do this and that ITE providers must carry out their own monitoring.
- *Promote tolerance in learners towards others' beliefs, cultures and backgrounds*: ITE programmes will need to address student teachers' own beliefs and values, develop their knowledge and understanding of cultural and religious issues (TTA, 2000) and educate them as to how to address these issues in schools.
- *Manage pupils well and insist on high standards of behaviour by positive reinforcement and tackling abuse and harassment*: ITE providers will need to make clear and explicit their own policies and practices on bullying and harassment and the serious nature of any breaches; as indicated above, there will need to be clear policies and procedures set up within school partnerships; and student teachers will need to explore how they can work with children to address bullying and harassment.
- *Plan effectively for the development of individual students and groups of students*: as indicated previously, students from minority ethnic groups (and other groups) have particular needs and concerns and ITE providers will need to address these in their planning; student teachers will need to develop approaches to curriculum planning in both the medium and short term which go beyond the current functional views of learning cycles to address the issues of how pupils' different social and cultural backgrounds impact on learning contexts and individual learning styles.
- *Use resources which give positive images of different cultures and backgrounds,*

drawing on students' experiences: many of the resources used in schools and ITE institutions are Eurocentric if not Anglo-centric and, as such, fail to celebrate the current social and cultural diversity: guidance such as that provided by the Runnymede Trust (1993) (in the process of revision) can provide student teachers with valuable guidance.

- *Promote security and identity by indicating high expectations and challenging stereotypes*: this is not simply a matter of political correctness but developing an institutional culture where all learners are expected to achieve and lack of achievement is not explained away by social or cultural background; ITE providers need to show they are to challenge and be challenged in relation to stereotypical expectations.
- *Using culturally sensitive language and being aware of cultural differences in gesture*: ITE providers will need to explore with student teachers the connotative meanings of culturally sensitive language and how misunderstandings of gesture can limit communication.
- *Utilise a range of approaches where students have difficulty learning*: ITE providers will need to make sure they model a range of different approaches to learning and discuss the impact this has on learners from different groups and those with varied learning styles.
- *Use time, support staff and other resources effectively*: student teachers will need to learn how to work collaboratively with learning support assistants, support students with disabilities through information and communication technology (ICT) and other resources and work with the guidance of specialist teachers such as those employed to support learners of English as an additional language (EMAG).
- *Appreciate their own cultural traditions and the diversities and richness of other cultures*: the content and methodological approach of the curriculum should celebrate cultural diversity (Runnymede Trust, 1993; Richardson and Wood, 1999).
- *Ensure equality of access and opportunity*: above all, both ITE providers and students must promote, *and be seen to promote*, 'education for all'. This must be one of the overarching principles of any programme of ITE.

If providers of ITE are to meet these demands, then there are three imperatives:

1. courses will need to be redesigned and revalidated with inclusion and equality of access and opportunity as an overarching principle;
2. in the same way as for teachers in schools, ITE staff are likely to need educating and this represents a major training initiative; and
3. this will need to have a very high, if not the highest priority, in ITE providers' development plans in the coming years as they will need to lead developments in this area.

The new Standards for ITE and their effectiveness in promoting inclusion

The Standards that *directly* address inclusion are shown in Table 4.1. Other Standards, particularly those in Section 1 concerned with professional values and practice, are also implicitly relevant to inclusion but have not been included here.

This is a much more comprehensive list than those contained in Circular 4/98 (DfEE, 1998) and therefore represents a considerable improvement. Important areas of inclusion are highlighted such as children with SEN, the support of children for whom English is an additional language, the valuing of diversity and the inclusion of children with behavioural emotional and social difficulties. The Standards outline many of the functional aspects of inclusion although, regrettably, the issues around social class are significantly understated. The draft handbook (TTA, 2001b) also provides useful support through the further elucidation of the Standards. What is noteworthy is that there is no direct reference to inclusion. The draft Standards (ibid.) required student teachers to have knowledge and understanding of the three principles of inclusion contained in National Curriculum 2000. Regrettably this has been omitted from the final version and one can only hope that it survives in the final handbook.

The TTA is caught on the horns of at least one dilemma – assessment. It has acted upon the responses received during the lengthy process of consultation undertaken to include a substantial section on professional values and practice; in terms of inclusion this is both significant and valuable. Again this is very much in line with the need in educating inclusive teachers to address issues of ideology and their own personal values and beliefs. However, these same values have to be assessed and one of the great problems is the difficulty of validly and reliably assessing values. To overcome this they have drafted many of the Standards in essentially observable, behavioural terms so that they can be judged against performance. The weakness of this approach is that ideas, values and beliefs are complex and often contradictory – a view that is held in one context is frequently opposed in another. (For example, many consider it acceptable to swear in the privacy of one's own home but not in front of a class of children.) The development and critical assessment of professional values cannot be something of the moment but will require the ongoing relationship between a skilled and reflective professional mentor and the aspiring student teacher. This is a central tenet of the apprenticeship model of training reflective practitioners (Schon, 1983).

Reynolds (2001, p. 471) makes reference to the view held in education in Northern Ireland that the following are teachers' key professional values:

> '... caring for children, enthusiasm for teaching, commitment to reflective practice, commitment to equality of opportunity and recognition of the worth of the education of the whole child.'

The TTA Standards indicate aspects of many of these without ever quite moving away from a rather mechanistic and behavioural view which may be perceived to be needed when keeping an eye to assessment and inspection. For example, in terms of the commitment to reflective practice, Standard 1.7 states

> 'They [the student teachers] are able to improve their own teaching, by evaluating it, learning from the effective practice of others and from evidence. They are motivated and are able to take increasing responsibility for their own professional development' (TTA, 2002, p. 6).

Table 4.1 Professional Standards for Qualified Teacher Status directly related to educational and social inclusion (TTA, 2002)

1.1	They have high expectations of all pupils; respect their social, cultural, linguistic, religious and ethnic backgrounds; and are committed to raising their educational achievement.
2.4	They understand how pupils' learning can be affected by their physical, intellectual, linguistic, social, cultural and emotional development.
2.6	They understand their responsibilities under the SEN Code of Practice, and know how to seek advice from specialists on less common types of special educational needs.
3.1.2	They use these teaching and learning objectives to plan lessons, and sequences of lessons, showing how they will assess pupils' learning. They take account of and support pupils' varying needs so that girls and boys, from all ethnic groups, can make good progress.
3.1.3	They select and prepare resources, and plan for their safe and effective organisation, taking account of pupils' interests and their language and cultural backgrounds, with the help of support staff where appropriate.
3.2.4	They identify and support more able pupils, those who are working below age-related expectations, those who are failing to achieve their potential in learning, and those who experience behavioural, emotional and social difficulties. They may have guidance from an experienced teacher where appropriate.
3.2.5	With the help of an experienced teacher, they can identify the levels of attainment of pupils learning English as an additional language. They begin to analyse the language demands and learning activities in order to provide cognitive challenge as well as language support.
3.3.1	They have high expectations of pupils and build successful relationships, centred on teaching and learning. They establish a purposeful learning environment where diversity is valued and where pupils feel secure and confident.
3.3.4	They differentiate their teaching to meet the needs of pupils, including the more able and those with special educational needs. They may have guidance from an experienced teacher where appropriate.
3.3.5	They are able to support those who are learning English as an additional language, with the help of an experienced teacher where appropriate.
3.3.6	They take account of the varying interests, experiences and achievements of boys and girls, and pupils from different cultural and ethnic groups, to help pupils make good progress.
3.3.14	They recognise and respond effectively to equal opportunities issues as they arise in the classroom, including by challenging stereotyped views, bullying or harassment, following relevant policies and procedures.

Source: TTA (2002).

One can foresee student teachers efficiently completing sheaves of proformas involving assessment, evaluation and lesson planning without ever significantly reflecting on how their own values and beliefs might have affected either this process or their approach to teaching and learning in the classroom. As Reynolds (2001, p. 475) puts it:

'We must develop teachers who are self-consciously aware of the values implicit in how they interact with pupils and how they fulfil their professional role. We need teachers

who can interrogate their practice by examining the values they are revealing an
matching their performance to a fuller range of criteria than those offered by the TTA

How, then, will the new Standards take us forward and where are they likely to come up short?

ITE programmes will need to contain a much greater functional focus on meeting the needs of a wide range of groups of pupils if students are to demonstrate competence in teaching, and this must be welcomed. It is also difficult to see how this will not have some impact on the attitudes and values discussed on courses but it is difficult to determine how large this impact will be. Certainly there appears no requirement to address the central issue of how schools' and teachers' attitudes have impacted on the learning and limited the attainments of particular groups within society.

ITE providers will also need to manage carefully the placement of students in schools. It is encouraging to see that theTTA have determined that student teachers should have experience of at least two schools. In practice this may not be enough given the range of contexts which the Standards require students to teach effectively. Geographical locality may also impact on the feasibility of this requirement given that some providers are some distance from urban conurbations. This requirement may present particular difficulties to primary postgraduate programmes where time in school is limited to 18 weeks. Schools and school-based mentors will need to take a significant, if not leading, role in the training of student teachers in inclusion. Many schools themselves are still coming to terms with the welter of initiatives in this area and the training of mentors may need to assume a higher priority.

As discussed previously, if the ability to reflect critically on professional values is essential to effective inclusion, then prospective student teachers will need to demonstrate a propensity to be able to do this, particularly those entering one-year programmes. In the trainee entry requirements reference is made to entrants *'possessing the appropriate personal and intellectual qualities to be teachers'* (TTA, 2002, R. 1.1). Whereas elsewhere the requirements in terms of literacy are made entirely explicit (R. 1.6) what is not made clear is the meaning of the term 'appropriate' in relation to personal, professional qualities – which has to be of at least equal significance. The requirement that all prospective students are interviewed, which in the draft Standards had been removed, is important; it is difficult to see how an assessment could be made as to a student's suitability without this. ITE providers may also wish to explore prospective students' ability for personal reflection through other strategies such as the review of case studies or discussion groups.

Finally, as indicated above, it is important to the development of inclusive education that student teachers from groups that are currently under-represented within the professior are encouraged to apply. It is disappointing to see no mention in the trainee entry requirements that ITE providers should ensure that their entry procedures do not disadvantage any of these groups. Also omitted is the need for ITE providers to review their entry criteria to make sure they fully recognise the capabilities students bring with them. For example, the ability to communicate fluently in a community language or an understanding of more than one culture would significantly support student teachers' ability to achieve at least five of the Standards in Table 4.1.

Conclusion

The new Standards do mark a move forward in terms of promoting inclusive education but, as I have indicated, still leave many issues not addressed. ITE providers will *have* to make some changes in terms of developing the skills, knowledge and understanding needed to achieve the Standards around the issues of inclusion but there is no requirement either to address the issue of inclusion directly or to encourage students to examine the ideologies that underpin theirs and others' educational practice. By not directly tackling inclusion they also fail to tackle the problematic nature of the issues surrounding it and the challenges that teachers are facing, and are likely to continue to face, in schools. The overall judgement on the Standards must be that they represent an inadequate response to the agenda of inclusion.

Two terms which are much in common usage are 'compliance' and 'promotion'. A common activity of ITE providers (and many others) is to determine whether they are compliant with statutory requirements. In essence this could mean that ITE programmes need only meet a minimum level of compliance. I am reminded of working some years ago on an assessment project where we realised that if we interpreted the criteria in terms of the minimum standard that pupils were expected to attain, my dog could achieve almost all Level I in Science Attainment Target 1. That is the danger of compliance. Promotion is concerned with the aspiration to achieve the highest standard and a recognition that the really important aspects of education are unbounded concepts. Inclusion is one of these concepts. It is important that we don't allow it to be denigrated, marginalised and ultimately forgotten.

References

Ainscow, M. (1997) Towards inclusive schooling, *British Journal of Special Education* 24: 3–6.

Carrington, B., Bonnett, A., Demaine, J., Hall, I., Nayak, A., Short, G., Skelton, C., Smith, F. and Tomlin, R. (2001) *Ethnicity and the Professional Socialisation of Teachers: Report to the Teacher Training Agency.* London: TTA.

Commission for Racial Equality (CRE) (2000) *Learning for All: Standards for Racial Equality in Schools.* London: CRE.

Centre for Studies in Inclusive Education (CSIE) (2002) *Working Towards Inclusive Education: Ten Reasons for Inclusion.* (http://inclusion.uwe.ac.uk/csie/10rsns.htm).

DFE (1993) Circular 14/93 *The Initial Training of Primary Teachers: New Criteria for Courses.* London: HMSO.

Department for Education and Employment (DfEE) (1997a) *Excellence in Schools.* London: HMSO.

DfEE (1997b) *Excellence for All Children: Meeting Special Educational Needs.* London: HMSO.

DfEE (1998) *Teaching: High Status, High Standards.* Circular 4/98. London: HMSO.

DfEE (1999) *Social Inclusion: Pupil Support.* Circular 10/99. London: HMSO.

Department for Education and Employment (DfEE) and Qualifications and Curriculum Authority (QCA) (1999) *The National Curriculum: Handbook for Primary Teachers in England, Key Stages 1 and 2*. London: HMSO.

Department for Education and Skills (DfES) (2001) *Special Educational Needs: Code of Practice*. London: HMSO.

Disability Rights Commission (DRC) (2002) *Disability Discrimination Act 1995, Part 4: Code of Practice for Schools: New Duties (from 2002) not to Discriminate against Disabled Pupils and Prospective Pupils in the Provision of Education and Associated Services in Schools, and in Respect of Admissions and Exclusions*. Barking: Disability Rights Commission.

Gillborn, D. and Mirza, H. S. (2000) *Educational Inequality: Mapping Race, Class and Gender – a Synthesis of Research Evidence*. London: OFSTED.

Hallam, S. and Castle, F. (2001) Exclusion from School: What Can Help Prevent It?, *Educational Review*, 53(2): p.169–79.

Hornby, G. (1999) Inclusion or delusion: can one size fit all?, *Support for Learning*. 14(4): p. 152–57.

Jones, R. (1999) *Teaching Racism or Tackling It? Multicultural Stories from White Beginning Teachers*. Stoke on Trent: Trentham Books.

Macpherson, W. (1999) *The Stephen Lawrence Report*. London: HMSO.

Office for Standards in Education (OFSTED) (2000) *Evaluating Educational Inclusion: Guidance for Inspectors and Schools*. London: OFSTED.

Parsons, C. (1999) Social inclusion and school improvement. *Support for Learning* 14(4): p. 179–83.

Reay, D. (2001) Finding or losing yourself? Working-class relationships to education. *Journal of Education Policy* 16(4): p. 333–46.

Reynolds, M. (2001) Education for inclusion, teacher education and the Teacher Training Agency Standards. *Journal of In-Service Education* 27(3): p. 465–76.

Richardson, R. and Wood, A. (1999) *Inclusive Schools, Inclusive Society: Race and Identity on the Agenda*. Stoke on Trent: Trentham Books.

Rogers, C. (1982) *A Social Psychology of Schooling*. London: Routledge & Kegan Paul.

Runnymede Trust (1993) *Equality Assurance in Schools: Quality, Identity, Society*. Stoke-on-Trent: Trentham Books.

Runnymede Trust (1998) *Improving Practice: A Whole School Approach to Raising the Achievement of African Caribbean Youth*. London: Central Books.

Schon, D. (1983) *The Reflective Practitioner*. London: Temple Smith.

Stenhouse, L. (1975) *An Introduction to Curriculum Research and Development*. London: Heinemann.

Teacher Training Agency (TTA) (2000) *Raising the Attainment of Minority Ethnic Pupils*. London: TTA.

TTA (2001a) *Standards for the Award of Qualified Teacher Status and Requirements for Initial Teacher Training: Report on the Responses to the Consultation of July 2001*. London: TTA.

TTA (2001b) *Handbook to Accompany the Standards for the Award of Qualified Teacher Status and Requirements for the Provision of Initial Teacher Training: Consultation Document*. London: TTA.

Department for Education and Skills (DfES) and Teacher Training Agency (TTA) (2002) *Qualifying to Teach: Professional Standards for Qualified Teacher Status and Requirements for Initial Teacher Training*. London: DfES/TTA.

UNESCO (1994) *The Salamanca Statement and Framework for Action on Special Needs Education* Paris: UNESCO.

Weiner, G. (2001) Social inclusion, responsible citizenship, social justice, equal opportunities: whatever happened to professional development? *Journal of In-Service Education* 27(3): p. 357–359.

Wilson, J. (1999) Some conceptual difficulties about 'inclusion'. *Support for Learning* 14(3): p. 110–112.

Section 2:
Qualifying to teach: putting the new requirements into practice

Over recent years there has been an increasing emphasis in schools on inclusion as a key principle. This has occurred particularly since the publication of the revised National Curriculum (DfEE, 2000) with its explicit statement encouraging schools to ensure access to the curriculum for all through appropriate expectations, objectives, teaching approaches, resources and support. The inclusion principle has been further endorsed in National Literacy Strategy and National Numeracy Strategy publications dealing with approaches for working with pupils with special educational needs (SEN) or those for whom English is an additional language (EAL) within whole-class and group teaching. The term 'inclusion' as used here goes beyond the idea of meeting different needs through special provision, often done previously as separate group teaching outside the classroom setting and requiring time to be lost from other curriculum activities. Teachers must look at the demands of all lessons across the subject range and set these against the specific needs of individuals or groups to ensure full access for all and enable them to be part of, not selectively excluded, from classroom work. This inevitably makes greater demands on the teacher in planning, resourcing and teaching, both in terms of knowledge and strategies to facilitate the wider range of pupil needs and learning approaches, and in relation to assessment and needs identification.

The high profile now being given to inclusion in schools is reflected in the recently published Standards to be met by those seeking Qualified Teacher Status (QTS) (DfES/TTA, 2002). This chapter considers the extent to which inclusion is emphasised as part of the new requirements and the demands this will then make on student teachers and on those who support and assess their development within initial teacher training and education (ITTE) partnerships. It will examine:

- expectations in relation to inclusion from 2002 and how this may differ from those in Circular 4/98 (DfEE, 1998);
- what changes in expectations and practice might be needed to enable student teachers to meet these requirements; and
- the implications for providers of ITTE.

From the initial Introduction to, and through each section of, *Qualifying to Teach* (DfES/TTA, 2002), the issue of inclusion is taken up; it is signalled, in particular, by the use of the word *all* to precede *pupils* as well as by much more specific reference to particular groups and needs. In the second paragraph of the Introduction to the new Standards, for example, it states that:

'Good teachers are always optimistic about what their pupils can achieve, whatever their background or circumstances. They understand that all their pupils are capable of significant progress and that their potential for learning is unlimited' (ibid. p. 2).

Section 1 on 'Professional values and practice' also begins with a key statement of the principle. Those awarded QTS must demonstrate that they:

> 'Have high expectations of all pupils; respect their social, cultural, linguistic, religious and ethnic backgrounds; and are committed to raising their educational achievement' (ibid. Standard 1.1).

By pointing to educational achievements as the outcomes in this more focused way this statement echoes, but goes beyond the parallel Standard in 'Other professional requirements' in Circular 4/98 (DfEE, 1998) in which student teachers must demonstrate that they 'are committed to ensuring that every pupil is given the opportunity to achieve their potential and meet the high expectations set for them'. However the messages about pupils' differing needs and facilitating their learning were all there in Circular 4/98. For example, there was recognition of inclusion as differentiation through more general statements about the need to identify 'clear teaching objectives and content appropriate to pupils being taught' (ibid. S. B4(a)i) and, in teaching, match 'approaches used to subject matter and the pupils being taught' (ibid. S. B4(k)ii). There were also some more specific statements, for example, that trainees had to demonstrate that they could promote progression through:

> 'identifying pupils who have special educational needs, including specific learning difficulties; are very able; are not yet fluent in English; and knowing where to get help in order to give positive targeted support' (ibid., S. B4(a)v).

and set 'high expectations for all pupils notwithstanding individual differences, including gender, and cultural and linguistic backgrounds' (ibid. S.B4(k)xiii). Familiarity with the SEN Code of Practice on the identification and assessment of SEN and implementing and keeping records on IEPs was also there (ibid. S. BB4l). Catering for EAL pupils, however, came through less in Annex A and was found in more detail in the English section – Annex C.

Whilst in the 4/98 Standards student teachers were to identify and, with help, target support in relation to differing needs, including EAL, as part of planning, teaching and assessing pupils, these requirements had less of a high profile. They were also less likely to have been interpreted to mean inclusion to the extent that the current National Curriculum (DfEE, 2000) emphasis on inclusion requires since they pre-dated this document and were not framed in such a direct manner. In addition, amidst the plethora of other Standards in 4/98 requiring assessment of student teacher competence, providers could be excused for seeing it in more general terms as ability to offer some differentiated work, in order to band together Standards to make them manageable for assessment purposes. Nevertheless, the main points were already there and simply needed mapping against the broader picture as a permeating aspect with little expansion, to give inclusion the higher profile suggested in the National Curriculum (ibid.).

Looking at the new document, Qualifying to Teach (DfES/TTA, 2002), the strand of inclusion now runs as a theme through each of the three sections: 1) 'Professional values and practice; 2) 'Knowledge and understanding'; and 3) 'Teaching' (which includes 3.1) planning, expectations and targets; 3.2) monitoring and assessment; and 3.3) teaching and class management.) It is included in a more explicit way than in Circular 4/98. As a core principle those gaining QTS are to respect, have high expectations for and raise achievements of *all* pupils (DfESS/TTA, 2002, S. 1.1). Knowledge and understanding includes not only the National Curriculum (with its inclusion statement), the National Literacy and Numeracy Strategy frameworks and the expectations and responsibilities under the SEN Code of Practice but also, in 2.4, *'how learning is affected by physical, intellectual, linguistic, social, cultural and emotional development'* – the additional categories here being linguistic and cultural links to learning. Across the sections there is also explicit reference to differing groups, including (now) recognition of differing religious and ethnic groups (SS. 1.1, 3.1.2, 3.3.6) as opposed, more broadly, to reference to pupils with differing *cultural and linguistic backgrounds.* Whereas before differing ability levels were indicated, now those underachieving are included (S. 3.2.4). Also recognised is the need to value diversity and differing interests, experiences and achievements as well as needs (SS. 3.1.3, 3.3.1, 3.3.6). Many of the Standards also refer to EAL, linguistic or cultural differences or the language demands of learning activities (SS. 2.4, 3.1.3, 3.2.5, 3.3.1, 3.3.5, 3.3.6) where previously EAL was given less of a profile. There is, moreover, a new recognition, given the inclusion now in mainstream schooling of pupils with more complex needs, that specialist advice may need to be sought for less common types of SEN (SS. 2.6). Student teachers are, in addition, expected to be able to recognise and respond to equal opportunities issues as they arise.

Newly Qualified Teachers are then expected to include all pupils, ensuring that interests and needs are identified, differentiating and giving access to the curriculum and assessing and monitoring needs and progress so that all pupils succeed. However there is a qualifying statement added to many of the relevant Standards to the effect that student teachers must demonstrate their knowledge or practical teaching ability in relation to aspects of inclusion with the help or guidance of experienced teachers or support staff. This seems to signal recognition of the complexity of this issue and the need to recognise that it is an aspect which cannot be mastered as a student teacher and will require further development after achieving QTS. Given this recognition one could question whether, in fact, this aspect of the Standards might not be best left to be considered as an induction Standard rather than assessed with such rigour for QTS.

Inclusion is a principle which ITTE providers are likely to want to endorse in general as a part of offering equal opportunities to pupils but it is important to look at the whole picture and the expectations this places on the student teachers and on those who work with them both in school and at their college or university. If inclusion is to have a higher profile and to permeate in this way, what changes may be needed in expectations and practice?

The higher profile of inclusion and demonstration of it in the classroom will need to be based on student teachers acquiring some considerable background knowledge and understanding, both in relation to the wide range of possible SEN and to EAL. This will have to be recognised as part of coursework, demonstrations of good practice, opportunities for practice and the assessment package.

The range of the knowledge base required becomes clear when one looks at the issues involved, for example, in just one subject area, English. SEN requirements may vary widely in relation to literacy and oracy and include a range of language development or processing difficulties – spoken and written, productive and receptive, including physical difficulties or dyslexia – with all the related effects on learning and difficulties in managing the language demands of English or other curriculum areas.

EAL and the role of other cultures in relation to English literacy and oracy will already be part of ITTE courses but the higher profile now for EAL will force a re-examination of what this must involve, how to cover it and where aspects will need to be located (for example, what should be covered through curriculum courses other than English). Course planning teams may need to consider, for example, the acquisition of English as an additional language and its development patterns; the role of other languages; dual language opportunities; positive models and prejudicial or racist language; text selection and giving access to texts and activities including use of information and communication technology (ICT); unpacking language demands of differing situations, texts, tasks and subjects; the effect of EAL on writing development and assessment of achievement; and many more aspects. Add to this gender issues and issues related to self-esteem and identity which link to language variety, bias and cultural patterns of communication, and the effect of all this on selection of texts and tasks, and you become aware that there is here a whole curriculum in addition to the basic teaching of English skills and knowledge to be addressed.

The needs of pupils with SEN and EAL will have to permeate throughout courses with coverage of them mapped across course elements. Discrete lectures or seminars cannot address the full range adequately. There are implications for all subject areas in relation to literacy and language across the curriculum and the demands on pupils' language as part of all planning, teaching and assessment in the inclusive classroom. There will also need to be explicit course content in subject areas and general professional studies, as well as provision for observation of good practice devoted to planning for and teaching pupils with these and other needs in an inclusive manner. Assessment – formative, diagnostic and summative – is also given a high profile through the requirements to identify and support pupils' needs and will need to be covered in theoretical and practical terms.

Clearly there are also differing levels of need in relation to SEN. Some children have less severe learning, physical and behavioural difficulties. These may require much less in terms of planning or of ways of giving access to the curriculum than those with more severe problems. Nevertheless specific knowledge of the difficulties, their impact on learning and approaches to engage these children will be needed and, in particular, ways to manage the learning experience within the classroom. This is an added layer of information needed in courses which may have covered the SEN Code of Practice, and some examples (perhaps through educational or general professional studies) and may now need to consider this generic area in more detail as well as look at it in relation to particular special needs and particular subjects.

From a different perspective 'inclusion' requirements present an added expectation on partnerships with placement schools – namely, that the student teachers have the opportunity to engage with at least a range of needs, albeit with the support and guidance of experienced teachers, if they are to be assessed on their ability to offer appropriate inclusive lessons. This raises an issue of entitlement, too, to ensure that each student teacher has the appropriate opportunities to learn about and demonstrate his or her competence. Courses will perhaps need to monitor the student teachers' experiences in relation to opportunities to engage with issues of inclusion of pupils with differing types of need.

The need to give adequate experience to the student teacher may require some change in policy for some classes in partnership schools. Previously student teachers may have taught the class without the more difficult pupils present because they were taken out for extra help, or the teacher used the time to give additional one-to-one support or because pupils were excluded to give the student teacher a chance to engage positively and develop management skills at a basic level before tackling the full class. There will now be an expectation that they plan for and manage the learning of all the pupils. The impact of setting, or of withdrawal of pupils for springboard groups, or additional literacy support, will need to be considered in enabling the student teacher to have adequate opportunity to develop and demonstrate knowledge and practice with pupils with a range of needs and abilities.

Pupils with quite severe difficulties are now likely to be found in school settings. Teachers, of course, develop their knowledge of these pupils' specific needs as and when the need arises. For student teachers, management of the learning of these pupils will be more strongly supported by teachers and assistants but there will, nevertheless, be a need for opportunities for these trainee teachers to gather the relevant information about how to tackle specific, more complex needs to facilitate inclusion. This is not always easy in the midst of a busy time in school.

The management of EAL pupils will need to be addressed for *all* student teachers, not easy in practice in areas such as the south west where these needs are less represented in the school population though there may be isolated EAL learners with their own particular problems of isolation. Again there is an entitlement issue and a need to track student teachers' experiences to ensure they have the appropriate opportunities to work with EAL pupils or to provide additional opportunities to supplement their teaching experiences.

What, then, are the implications for ITTE providers in designing courses and providing appropriate experiences and assessment opportunities in relation to the Standards? A clear need to integrate inclusion into all aspects of the courses is signalled. Contextualised approaches with input across the range of subject areas especially for primary student teachers, as well as generic information, will be needed. This will model good practice in its own right and provide the necessary opportunities for student teachers to gain the appropriate range of knowledge within subject areas, as well as in general terms. Providers could find ways to engage the student teachers in monitoring their growing knowledge and awareness of permeating themes related to inclusion, for example by having them keep a journal reflecting on the implications from differing input or subject areas. This could provide part of the assessment for the Standards.

To address knowledge of more severe problems it may be appropriate to offer input from specialists or other agencies such as representatives from the National Autistic Society or the British Epilepsy Association. Other more generic input might be gained through working internally with other university departments (for example, trainee psychologists), thus offering a common opportunity for professional development. Visits to special schools or special units might also be appropriate here.

Placement schools will need to be monitored in relation to the opportunities offered to:

- observe, teach and discuss examples of good inclusive practice;
- gain a range of experience (for example, to work with pupils with EAL or differing needs);
- provide appropriate support and training; and
- assess student teachers in this area of the Standards.

This may be difficult for smaller schools.

At the same time there may need to be consideration here of how to help student teachers to develop their confidence and ability to manage the whole class where there are considerable difficulties, especially in behavioural terms. Moderation and quality assurance in relation to assessment of student teachers will need to include consideration of this aspect of practice.

Mentor training will have to address the way inclusion is presented in school and any required opportunities for observation of practice and input to student teachers as well as support as they develop their practice. Inclusion will also need to be considered in relation to assessment of the Standards. Here there could well be issues of entitlement, expectation, parity and a need for quality assurance and moderation to ensure equal opportunities.

The need both to understand and practise inclusion of pupils with EAL creates special problems for providers in areas with more limited variety in cultural, linguistic or ethnic pupil backgrounds. Here providers may need to consider alternative experiences through shorter distanced placements, liaison with the LEA and making use of *'teaching in settings other than schools'* (DfES/TTA, 2002, R. 2.5). The need to provide and monitor a range of opportunities, and assess ability to operate inclusion, especially the teaching of pupils with EAL, will also challenge some of the providers of more flexible postgraduate routes and School-Centred Inital Teacher Training (SCITT) schemes.

Even with all this there are still some questions for ITTE providers to address. For example, how can what is now required be fitted into an already full programme for Professional Certificate in Education (PGCE) students, especially those undertaking Key Stages 2/3 courses? How can appropriate experiences be offered to all student teachers? There are also questions of interpretation. What is meant by *'identify and* support' (DfES/TTA, 2002, R. 3.2.4) differing needs or by *identify the levels of attainment of pupils learning English as an additional language*' (ibid., R. 3.2.5)? How much is expected or should be expected of student teachers? How effectively can it be assessed, given the range of needs? Is this added layer in fact requiring, in some cases, quite sophisticated knowledge and practical expertise inappropriate at this stage to pursue in detail to the point of assessment for QTS? Should providers perhaps be pressing for 'inclusion', in the more elaborate sense the Standards seem to indicate, as an area best assessed in the induction year?

Whatever the views of providers there is considerable work ahead to adjust courses and partnership work to include 'inclusion' with its higher profile, as detailed in the new Standards, and to fit it into already full courses in a meaningful way and assess it appropriately for those being awarded QTS by whatever route.

References

Department for Education and Employment (DfEE) (1998). *Teaching: High Status, High Standards*. Circular 4/98. London: DfEE.

DfEE (2000) *The National Curriculum*. London: DfEE/QCA.

Department for Education and Skills (DfES) and Teacher Training Agency (TTA) (2002) *Qualifying to Teach: Professional Standards for Qualified Teacher Status and Requirements for Initial Teacher Training*. London: DfES/TTA.

Chapter 6: Prospects for partnership in initial teacher training and education; implementing the new requirements

Phil Bassett

This chapter looks at the new Standards and requirements for the education and training of teachers in England, with a particular emphasis on the prospects for partnership. In considering the reasons that underlie the introduction of these new orders attention will be given to recent developments in the 'partnership with schools' model for initial teacher training and education (ITTE) and the way in which the new document recognises the strengths of such an approach. The chapter analyses the opportunities that are available within the new regulations and attends to issues that providers of ITTE will need to consider when reviewing their existing programmes. Finally, the chapter will give consideration to those elements that have received no attention in the new orders but are seen to have a significant impact on the quality and sustainability of this model.

There can be little doubt that few initiatives have had such an enormous impact on the preparation and training of teachers as the introduction of the partnership model. This is not to say that the formal involvement of schools has proceeded smoothly. On the contrary, only small numbers of schools 'signed-on' during the critical stages and the professional associations advocated caution in the face of a possible increase in workload for little remuneration (Ring, 1995; UCET, 1995). The situation has, however, improved considerably and now significant numbers of schools in England and Wales work with ITTE providers to prepare the next generation of teachers.

The initial steps towards formalising the relationship between schools and ITTE providers were taken by the government with the introduction of Circular 9/92 (DfE, 1992) and Welsh Office Circular 35/92 (Welsh Office, 1992) for the training of secondary teachers. This required schools to assume greater responsibility for the training of teachers through collaborative or 'partnership' agreements with ITTE providers. The Education Act 1994 not only established the partnership model for teacher training but also introduced an increased role for schools by permitting them to take the lead, making use of higher education staff only where they believed their contribution to be desirable. During this two-year period, the schools had moved from a support role in ITTE to at least an 'equal partner' position, which would be strengthened by subsequent regulations (DfEE, 1998a; 1998b; Welsh Office, 1998). This move to empower schools has been supported, in the main, by the traditional providers as they recognise the significant contribution that schools make to the training process and the value that such close working relationships can add to their ITTE courses. The partnership model has moved the placement elements of ITTE courses from a simple 'teaching practice' approach where classroom teachers had little formal input to the design, monitoring and assessment of the trainee's experience to a 'school experience' approach that embraces many more of the aspects of the teacher's role within the 'life' of the school. In an attempt, initially to meet legislative requirements, schools and higher education institutions (HEIs) have developed, in partnership, clear roles and responsibilities for participating staff and efficient processes to prepare and support trainees to meet the Standards for Qualified Teacher Status (QTS) and to enter the profession.

Within the ten-year life of the partnership approach to ITTE, there have been numerous tensions when HEIs have been forced to comply with initiatives or legislation that have been introduced with little or no consultation. Perhaps the greatest strength of the new document (DfES/TTA, 2002) is that it has been produced with a 'cast of thousands'. Throughout the last year, groups of contributors drawn from all sectors within education have been given the opportunity to air their opinions, draft statements and respond to initial findings to ensure that the document reflects the views of the providers. As a contributor to the requirements for the ITTE section (ibid.), it was apparent that notice was taken of the opinions expressed during the numerous working sessions. Again, those reading the consultation document (TTA, 2001) will, when comparing it with the final document, see that changes have been made as a result of the responses submitted. This receptive approach to the providers will be welcomed and should be sustained to ensure that the implementation process is evolutionary, building on good practice which is supported by an evidence base.

I intend to explore the process through which the new requirements for ITTE have been decided and to explore the content as it relates to the promotion of partnership. At this point, it should be mentioned that the views expressed in the following pages, whilst essentially my own, are also the result of a frantic period of e-mailing colleagues within the Association for Partnerships in Teacher Education for their immediate reflections on the new document. As a result of their replies, it would be fair to say that the new requirements have been received favourably but not unequivocally.

Initially, it is clear that this revision of the requirements for QTS builds on the foundation laid in earlier legislation to secure the partnership model for ITTE programmes. Requirement 3.1 (DfES/TTA, 2002) states the need for providers to involve schools in the planning and delivery of programmes and the selection and assessment of the trainee teachers. There is little here to cause concern, philosophically, for HEI providers as this represents elements of the current situation and would be recognised by those partici-pating in provision as 'good practice'. The difficulty, however, lies in the need to resource these requirements. To date, HEIs have managed this in a variety of ways, from direct payment to schools to a reliance on the goodwill of school staff. Within this range, numerous creative solutions have been developed but such understandings often make for tenuous or temporary arrangements that leave the provider with little guarantee that requirements will be met 'the next time around'. Although every effort is made by providers to comply with the existing requirements, the extent to which each is able to ensure that all these aspects are met is questionable. Therefore, simply reiterating the demand with no attention to the resource requirement is unlikely to achieve a more consistent compliance.

The development of R. 3 introduces little that is new in terms of the present partnership model for the majority of providers. Whilst this may be seen as again emphasising vital aspects of the existing partnerships, the expectation may well fall short of the reality. Certainly, the majority of partnership documents contain sections that make clear the role and responsibilities assigned to each participant within the partnership. Equally, there will be no difficulty in designing documents which *'set out arrangements for preparing and supporting all staff involved in training'* (ibid. R. 3.2). The difficulty will be with implementing the arrangements unless the resources are made available to provide such support. Research studies have shown that participating staff value and welcome the opportunity to receive initial and ongoing training (Williams and Soares, 2000) but that access to programmes is limited by time restraints (Geen *et al.*, 2000). Again, providers have offered solutions to the problems of access by accrediting mentor training courses and delivering low-cost or free in-service education and training (INSET) packages. However, school-based mentors are often unable to avail themselves of these opportunities when supply-teacher costs cannot be met by their school and they are reluctant to attend twilight or weekend provision. It is a concern for providers that they are unable to encourage previously trained mentors to attend regular refresher, developmental and updating sessions but a serious worry that many school-based staff members will act as mentors to trainee teachers without having themselves received any training at all.

The issues surrounding the provision of training for those participating in the partnership should not be dismissed lightly. Whereas the majority of providers will design their programmes with representatives from schools, the transmission of the programme's requirements to all participants is difficult to achieve without an effective method of dissemination. By implication, the 'design committee' is likely to include only a small number of people, but their decisions will involve all staff and trainees participating in the programme. Providers have attempted various methods of disseminating the information to all participants, and many partnership documents contain detailed information about the entire programme. Such an approach, however, requires every individual to read and understand the details of the scheme if coherence is to be achieved. Without an understanding of the entire programme, there is a danger that the participant will devote attention only to those elements that are seen as relevant to their role or aspects that fall within their responsibility. This will, in turn, fragment the programme and possibly restrict opportunities for the trainee. Regular training programmes would provide a means for the dissemination of information, the evaluation of implementation procedures and the opportunity to revise practice.

The issue of resources features prominently within the partnership model for ITTE from the perspective of the providers and of the government. In a survey of school-based training, Her majesty's Inspectors (HMI) (DES, 1991) recognised the validity of the concerns expressed by HEIs over the funding issues associated with the provision and monitoring of placements for the trainee teachers:

> *'Apart from staff salaries, expenditure associated with student experience in schools makes the largest demand on the institution's initial training budget ... Traditionally, school-based aspects of training have rested on an ill-defined principle of mutual benefit, with no money changing hands. Increasingly, as schools take responsibility for their own budgets, that principle is being challenged ... If teachers make a more substantial and formal contribution to training as opposed to simply providing teaching practice placements, a proper value will need to be placed on it.'*

Circulars 9/92 and 35/92 introduced the requirement for providers to transfer resources to the schools, and this issue was given additional attention in Circular 14/93 (DfE, 1993), where it was made clear that the payment to schools was in recognition of their increased contribution '... *over and above their existing commitment to teacher training'*. This obligation has remained constant in successive circulars and the new document requires that providers *'make clear how resources are divided and allocated between partners'*. Although not a new concept, the statement is now different from the initiatory interpretation and may be taken to imply that the allocation should be based on a model of cost analysis. Unfortunately, this could reopen partially healed wounds for many providers who would agree that the resource transferred to schools is insufficient to meet the direct costs of provision but that the unit of resource received allows little room for improved payment. Moreover, evidence is plentiful to support the view that partnerships between schools and providers bring benefits that cannot and should not be identified solely in terms of financial value (Geen *et al.*, 2000). What has not been addressed within the documents to date is the use made of the resources transferred from the provider to the school. Although Circulars 9/92 and 35/92 required the transfer of funding from HEIs to schools accommodating students, there is no obligation on governors to guarantee that it is actually spent on teacher training provision. Successive documents have made little or no reference to the way in which the school should use this increased resource and, unlike other aspects that have been developed by successive documents, this component has been ignored. If there had been a genuine desire to ensure that the resources transferred were used to support the trainee teacher, then both this and the transparency of allocation could have been included within the revised statement.

Perhaps the most significant change promoted within this revision of Circular 4/98 is the necessity for all providers to meet the same requirements for ITTE courses. This change ensures that there are now consistent expectations that must be addressed for courses delivered by HEIs, the Open University, consortia for School-Centred Initial Teacher Training (SCITT), Graduate and Registered Teacher Programmes (G/RTP), modular, flexible and part-time courses. The new requirements make it clear that all trainees '...*must have experience in at least two schools'* (DfES/TTA, 2002, R 2.5). Whilst this is not a new development for the more traditional HEI providers, it may represent a challenge for those providing alternative routes to QTS such as the G/RTP. The inclusion of this requirement may be seen as a response to those, like Wragg (1990), who believe that training based in a single school is lacking '... *both breadth of experience and access to research, reflection and theoretical frameworks'* (Foster, 2001). However, the statement does little to clarify the length of time that constitutes 'experience' in each school. In existing programmes, this has been interpreted widely from a week or two to an equal division of the total time requirement for each of two placements. The determination to ensure consistency of requirements across all provision is evidenced further within this section by the inclusion of the need to '... *prepare trainee teachers to teach across at least two Key Stages ...* ' (DfES/TTA 2002 R2.4). There is, however, no stated expectation in terms of length of time to be devoted to each Key Stage nor any explicit need to provide a placement for each of the two Key Stages. The implementation of the requirement appears to be left to the discretion of individual providers.

The obvious desire to avoid a prescriptive approach is evident in the continuation of R. 2.5: *'Teaching in settings other than schools may also count towards these totals, [the number of weeks a trainee spends being trained in schools for each programme]'.* Adopting this approach allows individual providers to interpret the statement and recognise the range of experience that trainees bring to their programme. Alternatively, the statement may be seen to encourage providers to be more creative in their design of the 'teaching' experiences they offer to trainees. If this is the correct interpretation of the requirement, then the door could be ajar for the offering of innovative experiences. This is not an entirely new development, as an earlier version of this flexibility was offered to providers when the time that trainees spend in schools was increased to their current levels. The opportunity that such an allowance presents, however, must be addressed with reference to the remaining requirements, and programme designers must ensure that the experiences are complementary to those gained in the school setting in order that trainees may meet the Standards for QTS.

The move to establish programmes that are adaptable to meeting the needs of individuals is a theme that has gained momentum during the past decade. Initially, attempts to provide individual training programmes for the award of QTS were not attributed directly to the HEI providers. Rather they were seen as a means of removing control for the training of teachers from the HEIs: *'... a strategy to nullify the role of HE in the preparation of teachers'* (Fish, 1995). The 'birth' of such programmes came with the introduction of the Licensed Teacher and Articled Teacher Schemes (DES, 1989), which began operation in 1990. Impetus for this development was provided by the introduction of the SCITT potential in the government's proposals for the reform of ITTE (DfE, 1993) and a number of school-centred consortia were formed to offer, and some continue to offer, programmes. In 1996, the Teacher Training Agency (TTA) proposed the introduction of the G/RTP as a means of providing *'... a tailor-made training route ...'* (TTA, 1996). This has now replaced the Licensed Teacher and Articled Teacher schemes and has enjoyed considerable success in terms of recruitment. The scheme has grown from modest numbers during the early years of operation to over 2,000 candidates presently enrolled. It is against this background that the requirement for all providers to *'ensure that training takes account of individual needs'* (DfES/TTA, 2002, R. 2.3) is set. Moreover, this should not be read in isolation from the previously discussed R. 2.5 that emphasises the accreditation of previous experience.

At first sight, the construction of individual programmes for trainees within a large cohort may appear to be a daunting and onerous task. For those involved with the G/RTP scheme, however, lessons have been learned and the experience of conducting a 'needs analysis' against the Standards may be no less demanding than the existing expectations for subject audits. Perhaps the early attention to assessment against the Standards would be beneficial in emphasising to trainees the importance of a self-critical and evidence-based approach towards measuring their progress. This would assist with the formative compilation of the Career Entry Profile (CEP) and establish good habits at an early stage of their professional development. For many providers, this approach to recording the progress of individual trainees will not be burdensome as many have embryonic or established systems in place. It is not difficult to see ways in which such systems could be modified to account for the results of an initial analysis of need. Indeed, this approach reflects the demands that are placed on trainees when they engage in the assessment of pupils for the setting of learning targets. Moreover, given the change in circumstances of many studying in higher education today as compared with a decade ago, the opportunity to receive exemption from certain elements of their programme will free them to engage in other activities. Certainly, the need to seek employment during their period of study is a demand that affects a considerable number of current students and such flexibility may prove essential for some if they are to continue their studies in higher education.

The aspects addressed to this point have attended to the requirements section of the new legislation and have discussed their impact on the ways in which the partnership model may respond. It would be too naïve to believe that the influence on partnership will be restricted to this section. Obviously, changes to the Standards and to the essential philosophical premise of the programme will have a considerable effect upon the way in which the partnership will operate to meet such reorientation or possible reconstruction. If the understanding is that the partnership will be the vehicle through which the aims of the programme are achieved, then it is essential for designers to consider the implications of change to their existing model. It is equally important for those designing the legislation to consider the effect that their requirements will have on the efficiency of the national partnership approach to ITTE.

The Introduction to the new document establishes within the first few pages the flexibility that is offered for the design of courses:

> 'These Standards are a rigorous set of expectations and set out the minimum legal requirement. We know that many primary teacher trainers will choose to supplement this minimum by continuing to offer a subject or phase specialism. Other trainers may choose to provide additional training which develops trainee teachers' knowledge and skills...' (DfES/TTA, 2002).

Examples of the range of ways in which providers may choose to supplement the minimum requirements are given and include: special education needs; personal, social and health education and citizenship; specialism in a non-National Curriculum subject; training to meet the Standards for further education and training relevant to the needs of a religion or for working in multilingual classrooms. This diversity of opportunity for programme designers is welcomed and the topics identified will be seen as important, but the varying programme supplements may place an additional strain on the partnership model. Schools often work in partnership with more than one provider. The difficulty of ensuring that the school-based staff are conversant with the programme documentation has already been discussed. If programmes differ considerably in the emphasis given to certain areas, individual schools may decide that the complexities of managing different providers' programmes is too great and may then decide to limit their collaboration to a single provider. Alternatively, schools with a particular area of expertise may choose to offer their services to the provider whose programme reflects their specialism and cease to offer placements to their traditional provider. For some schools, the additional demands of the new requirements may prove to be too burdensome and they may withdraw from collaboration altogether.

In an attempt to promote even closer working alliances with schools and by recognising '... *the essential contribution that schools and other settings make to initial teacher training*' (DfES/TTA, 2002), the government is ensuring that schools have a considerable influence over the nature of the programme offered. Within this revised version of the requirements for ITTE, however, there are increased expectations on the contribution from the school. The Standards section of the new document contains some nine references to trainee teachers being able to deliver subjects or aspects with the help of teachers, colleagues and/or support staff. In the majority of existing partnership arrangements such an expectation exists; however, the new document makes this understanding explicit and may have implications for quality assurance procedures. If a trainee teacher is not provided with '... *guidance from an experienced teacher where appropriate*' (ibid.) and the Standard is not met, then the appropriateness of the placement may become an issue. Obviously, not all schools will be in a position to provide the full range of support across all the areas identified within the document or with the distinctive supplement of the individual programme. The concern is that, if the expectation on schools becomes too great, then some schools, particularly those with small numbers of pupils and a small staff, may feel they are unable to meet the requirements and withdraw from the partnership. The special case of the small school's involvement in partnership has been recognised for some time and it has been demonstrated that what may be lost in terms of breadth of expertise is more than compensated for in other areas (Sanders, 1995). For these schools in particular, the demands of supporting trainee teachers in the subjects identified within S. 2.1b may be excessive.

The issues addressed above must be related to the introduction of S. 3.2.5 (DfES/TTA, 2002) which requires trainee teachers to '... *identify the levels of attainment of pupils learning English as an additional language.*' Again, it would be difficult to argue against the exigency for teachers to be capable of supporting pupils with these needs, but the necessity for all trainee teachers to be so equipped could be questioned. Perhaps this is an area for the qualified teacher to gain expertise as part of his or her programme for continued professional development once he or she has achieved mastery of the teaching of literacy. Whether this view is acceptable or not is immaterial to the demand that such a requirement will make on the provision of placements within a partnership. For some providers, this will not be a difficult placement to organise for their trainee teachers to gain the relevant experience to supply evidence of meeting the Standard. It is unlikely, however, that all providers will be in such a position and it must be assumed that for some programmes this will be addressed within the college-based element of the programme rather than in the school setting. If trainee teachers need the direct experience of working with pupils learning English as an additional language, then the flexibility offered by the phrase 'schools and other settings' will allow providers to make use of a variety of contexts outside that of the school setting to meet this requirement. If the Standard becomes tied to the school setting, then the difficulties faced by partnership administrators in securing sufficient opportunities for trainee teachers to develop expertise in some subjects, for example information and communication technology (ICT), may be further exacerbated.

Inevitably, any analysis of a new requirement will address areas of perceived difficulty when undertaken by those charged with its implementation. The document has been compiled as a result of extended consultation and has built on the secure foundations laid by previous statutory orders for the further development of the partnership model. Much of what is recognised as good practice in the operation of partnerships for ITTE has been included in the document. Moreover, opportunities have been created to encourage innovative practice with the agreement that:

> 'OFSTED will base its inspections on the statutory requirements ... OFSTED will not inspect against non-statutory guidance contained in the Handbook' (DfES/TTA, 2002).

Indeed, the deliberate lack of specification within the Standards and requirements supports the introductory comments that:

> 'They allow providers autonomy in deciding how they will organise their training and respond to individual trainee teachers' needs. They do not set a curriculum, nor do they specify how training should be organised and run' (DfES/TTA, 2002).

Inevitably, there will be unease amongst providers who must respond by interpreting the demands in the revision of their programmes and some will view the lack of direction in certain areas as unhelpful. Equally, some providers will be ready to experiment with the content of their courses, selecting areas to supplement their provision and engineering a fit for the needs of their particular context. If this is the case, then programme diversity will occur rapidly and the distinctive nature of programmes will emerge.

At this point in the analysis, it is worth while giving consideration to those areas that not only lack specific detail but also receive no attention in the actual document. Certainly, the greatest constraint on the development of the partnership model is the lack of funding available to support mentors in fulfilling their obligations to the trainee teachers as detailed in their partnership agreement responsibilities (Geen et al., 2000; 2001). Fundamentally, partnerships are under-resourced. This has been recognised by numerous research studies (Griffiths and Owen, 1995; UCET, 1995) and also by the inspectorate:

> 'HEIs and schools are at different stages in the development of mentoring in their various partnerships. If quality of provision and standards are to improve further, there is a need for more funding for the training of mentors, and quality assurance needs to be developed further' (OHMCI, 1998).

The Green Papers (DfEE, 1998b; Welsh Office, 1999) proposed that schools should be funded directly but gave no indication of the amount of funding each school would receive:

> 'We intend to review funding arrangements to ensure that they recognise the role of schools as equal partners. In particular, we will consult on the case for funding the

higher education/school partnership directly rather than channelling funding for partner schools through higher education institutions' (DfEE, 1998b).

Given the varied nature of each provider's programme and the use made of the time spent in schools, such an approach would be difficult to administer. Of greater interest is that this proposal was made with no explanation of the reasons which gave rise to the view and that no suggestions were offered of ways in which such a model would be implemented. Certainly, the administration of partnership represents a significant cost for the majority of HEI providers, but the direct payment of funds to schools could stifle some of the creative solutions that have been applied in compensating for under-funding to date. It is not surprising, therefore, that this suggestion has not been revived.

There can be little doubt that the most serious omission relates to the obligation placed on the individual sectors for the development of partnership. The document now expects that all providers will meet the requirement to work in partnership with schools but makes no reference to the need for schools to work in partnership with providers. Whilst it is recognised that the arguments for and against the adoption of such a position evoke emotive responses from all sectors of education, the fact remains that the onus is still upon providers to secure partnerships with schools. Such a position does little to address the concerns of providers when schools may withdraw from agreements as the result of staff changes, inspection demands and other reasons, leaving the HEI to count the costs of training, documentation and revised placement allocations. The perpetuation of a system which requires one partner to comply with legislative requirements and the other with the right to opt in or not is unlikely to encourage the effective development of 'equal partnership'. It may be paralleled by the farm animals' desire for a cooked breakfast, where the pig is committed totally but the hen only makes a contribution!

In summary, the new requirements recognise the achievements of providers and schools in developing an effective partnership model for ITTE. They build on the sound foundations already laid and appear to encourage further experimentation to allow for distinctive programme construction, restricting the parameters of Office for Standards in Education (OFSTED) inspection to the statutory section whilst providing additional support through the handbook and example materials. The introduction of a standardised set of requirements for all providers is to be welcomed and will ensure that a minimum entitlement for trainee teachers is established. Unfortunately, the opportunity to address the main inhibitor to partnership development has not been tackled and the issues surrounding the funding of the model will continue to be a cause of concern.

References

Department of Education and Science (DES) (1991) *School-based Initial Teacher Training in England and Wales: A report by H.M.Inspectorate.* London: HMSO.

Department for Education (DfE) and Welsh Office (1992) *Initial Teacher Training (Secondary Phase).* DFE Circular 9/92, WO Circular 35/92. London: DfE.

Department for Education (DfE) (1993) *The Initial Training of Primary School Teachers: New Criteria for Courses.* Circular 14/93. London: HMSO.

Department for Education and Welsh Office (1993) *The Government's Proposals for the Reform of Initial Teacher Training*. London: DfE.

Department for Education and Employment (DfEE) (1996) *Graduate Teacher Programme: Consultation Paper*. London: DfEE.

DfEE (1998a) *Teaching: High Status, High Standards*. Circular 4/98. (London, DfEE).

DfEE (1998b) *Teachers Meeting the Challenge of Change*. London: HMSO.

Department for Education and Skills (DfES) and Teacher Training Agency (TTA) (2002) *Qualifying to Teach: Professional Standards for Qualified Teacher Status and Requirements for Initial Teacher Training*. London: DfES/TTA.

Fish, D. (1995) *Quality Mentoring for Student Teachers: A Principled Approach to Practice*. London: David Fulton.

Foster, R. (2001) The graduate teacher route to QTS: motorway, by-way or by-pass? Unpublished paper delivered at the British Educational Research Association Conference.

Geen, A., Bassett, P. and Douglas, L. (2000) Benefits and costs: the impact of partnership in initial teacher education upon secondary schools in south-east Wales. *The Welsh Journal of Education* 9(2).

Geen, A., Bassett, P. and Douglas, L. (2001) Preparing student-teachers to assess pupils' achievements. *Westminster Studies in Education* 24.

Griffiths, V. and Owen, P. (eds.) (1995) *Schools in Partnership*. London: Paul Chapman Publishing.

Office of Her Majesty's Chief Inspector of Schools in Wales (OHMCI) (1998) *Mentoring in Initial Teacher Training: Secondary Phase: A Good Practice Document*. Cardiff: OHMCI.

Ring, K. (1995) Implications for schools of recent changes in initial teacher education: a National Union of Teachers viewpoint. In V. Griffiths and P. Owen (eds.) *Schools in Partnership*. London: Paul Chapman Publishing.

Sanders, S. (1995) Partnership with small primary schools. In V. Griffiths and P. Owen (eds.) *Schools in Partnership*. London: Paul Chapman Publishing.

TTA (2001) *Standards for the Award of Qualified Teacher Status and Requirements for the Provision of Initial Teacher Training: Consultation Response Booklet*. London: TTA.

Universities Council for the Education of Teachers (UCET) (1995) Survey reported in *The Times Educational Supplement* 20 January.

Welsh Office (1998) *Requirements for Courses of Initial Teacher Training*. Circular 13/98. Cardiff: Welsh Office.

Welsh Office (1999) *The BEST for Teaching and Learning*. Cardiff: Welsh Office.

Williams, A. and Soares, A. (2000) *The Power of Partnership: a Study of the Role of Higher Education in Secondary Postgraduate Initial Teacher Training*. London: Association of Teachers and Lecturers.

Wragg, T. (1990) The two routes into teaching. In M. Booth *et al.* (eds.) *Partnership in Initial Teacher Training*. London: Cassell Educational.

Introduction

This purpose of this chapter is to consider the implications of the revised standards and regulations for the award of Qualified Teacher Status (QTS) (DfES/TTA, 2002) for processes of assessment. As part of the consultation surrounding the development of the new requirements, a draft non-statutory handbook was published (TTA, 2001). This contained a code of practice for the assessment of the Standards. Whilst at the time of writing the final version of the code of practice has not been published, it is argued that the principles outlined and practice advocated in the draft document provide providers with some helpful direction as they consider their practice in this area and also raise some interesting issues for consideration. This chapter utilises the code of practice for assessment in the draft document in the sense that, whatever the final version, the code encapsulates some key indicators of Teacher Training Agency (TTA) thinking in this area.

It is certainly the case that some considerable variation has developed over a number of years in how initial teacher training and education (ITTE) providers assess their students. Work such as the 'Modes of Teacher Education' research project has demonstrated this variation, citing differences in course structure, the curriculum, the personnel involved in teaching and assessment, and the ways in which theoretical and practical knowledge are integrated (Furlong et al., 2000). Inspections of ITTE have reported more than once on issues surrounding assessment against the Standards, for example, in the Primary Follow-up survey when the Office for Standards in Education (OFSTED) reported on the

> 'need to ensure that the assessment of all trainees against the standards for QTS is comprehensive, rigorous and accurate' (1999, p. 9).

It could be argued that there are two, sometimes conflicting, processes in action contributing to the education of a student teacher. The student is first following a programme that has been validated by some form of institution. Professional Certificate in Education (PGCE) and undergraduate ITTE students are all following a course subject to the regulations of a Higher Education, or equivalent, institution or body. Secondly, the student is progressing towards and ultimately hoping to achieve QTS when assessed against the standards set out by the TTA.

Added to this is the great variation in provider types. Providers range from university departments of education (UDEs) and other higher education institutions (HEIs) with significant teacher education operations (for example, colleges of higher education and university colleges, many of which have their roots as 'teacher training colleges') to School-Centred Initial Teacher Training groups (SCITTs) and the Graduate and Registered Teacher Preparation (G/RTP) programmes.

Variation in manoeuvrability within and around institutional regulations and variation in size and type of provider inevitably result in variation in traditions as to the purpose of assessment and in procedures used when assessing. It was of no surprise to the teacher education sector that the TTA became keen to develop work already being carried out elsewhere on developing a consensus on the purpose of assessment in ITTE and an agreement as to what procedures ought to ensure as a minimum.

An examination is made here of the various approaches adopted by a number of providers with respect to each of the sections in the draft code of practice on assessing the standards.

The purpose of assessment in ITTE

Assessing to the Standards

The code of practice suggests that assessment to the Standards is likely to evidence students' 'progress towards' and 'achievement of' the Standards. Ultimately the Standards must be evidenced at a final summative or synoptic assessment point after which QTS can be recommended and the Career Entry Profile (CEP) contents agreed. Much emphasis is placed, however, on the ways in which students might be supported through formative assessment approaches as they progress towards their final achievement of the Standards. Writing at the time when the term 'competency' was replaced by 'standard' and referring specifically to the terminology of Circular 10/97 (DfEE, 1997), which heralded the present Standards, Sixsmith (1998, p. 188) observed that:

> 'The standards, in the way in which they are worded, appear to be criteria. The process of assessing students by the standards would appear to be criterion-referenced. Students will achieve the standards or not…'

It is the case that students may progress towards the Standards setting targets through assessment that is formative in function, but that the ultimate achievement of each individual Standard is criterion-referenced in type and summative in function.

Writing for students in ITTE, Hyland and Jacques (2000, p. 3) give a useful reminder that the Standards (as set out in Circular 4/98 – DfEE, 1998b) are not the only assessment criteria that experienced professionals might use in their assessment:

> 'Underpinned as they are by statutory powers and backed by all the appearance of official authority, they tend to give an appearance of universal agreement on what is required of teachers. You will soon learn that there is always some disagreement amongst teachers and those who train them over just which knowledge, skills and attitudes are essential for the Newly Qualified Teacher (NQT), or indeed for the experienced teacher. The requirements of Circular 4/98 are by no means the only "standards" which we might wish to consider, nor the only version of what it might mean to be an effective beginning teacher.'

Assessment for differing reasons

Brown et al. (1997, p. 7) remind us of the often dominating importance of assessment in defining the student experience:

'Assessment defines what students regard as important, how they spend their time and how they come to see themselves as students Students take their cues from what is assessed rather than from what lecturers assert is important. Put rather starkly: If you want to change student learning then change the methods of assessment.'

It is increasingly argued by providers that the criterion-referenced nature of the Standards, and the quantity of them, have resulted in the Standards driving much of the assessment of the courses that students follow. Assessment opportunities are seen as opportunities to evidence progress towards or achievement of specific Standards and specific assignments on ITTE programmes have been re-crafted accordingly.

In undergraduate ITTE courses there are some assessment pressures that are not present in the same way on professional graduate routes. On an undergraduate course a student is following a degree programme and is being assessed against the criteria as laid out in the relevant degree documentation as well as working to evidence the Standards. The purpose of assessment in ITTE is not, therefore, only to facilitate evidencing of the Standards but it can also be to obtain a degree or a PGCE.

If we examine the 'purpose of assessment' with respect to each assessment point then we can focus much more specifically on how we work students through the Standards. At this level we begin to examine how the Standards might be 'mapped' against the assessment experiences of students. At each assessment point a decision is made as to whether the assessment of the student provides evidence of progress towards or achievement of any of the Standards. The assessor has to be clear as to why the assessment is taking place and to be clear as to whether assessment criteria are:

- unrelated to the Standards;
- related to the Standards but also for other reasons (e.g. degree course-related criteria); or
- related only to the Standards.

Each provider has considered the degree to which their programmes have had to have the Standards 'mapped against' their existing provision or the degree to which they want to revalidate programmes 'from scratch' to reflect the Standards as a fundamental assessment regime that has to underpin the 'shape' and timing of assessment across the whole programme.

Procedures for the assessment of ITE students

The code of practice suggests four areas of procedure where providers act to assure quality of assessment. These are procedures:

1. for the design, approval and management of assessment;
2. to ensure involvement of professionals from across the partnership;
3. to ensure sharing of assessment strategies across all assessors to ensure consistency; and
4. for review and updating/improvement in line with internal and external changes to requirements.

Design, approval, management, review and improvement of assessment practice

Procedures for the design, approval and management of assessment strategies vary from provider to provider, but inevitably are largely determined by internal regulatory and quality assurance systems. The same can be said, at least to a degree, about the procedures for review and improvement of assessment strategies:

> 'The reality as to how assessment is designed across a whole programme and then man-aged and reviewed varies from institution to institution. Typically, initial approval and periodic re-approval tends to be fairly general in its nature as teachers and assessors are rightly keen to leave some freedom or flexibility for those who are to assess stu-dents ''on the ground''. Irrespective of institutional quality assurance and course valida-tion systems, it is essential therefore that providers develop and support a culture of sharing good assessment practice and a system at the operational level for questioning the practices used and updating them when relevant.'

Assessment training within and across the partnership

The range of assessment strategies used in an ITTE setting is very wide but has traditionally been developed and managed wholly from within the institution itself. There has been some significant variation from institution to institution as to the degree to which school-based assessors have been seen as 'part of the assessment team'. It is now the case that mentors, leading mentors and other school-based assessors have become central to the operation of providers' assessment systems. OFSTED inspection of ITTE has resulted in a very focused emphasis on the role of the wider partnership in assessing students and has helped drive providers forward in their improvement of partnership-wide systems and procedures.

'Ideal' models of partnership

The second Modes of Teacher Education (MOTE) project (between 1993 and 1996) has led to the suggestion that collaborative or complementary 'ideal' models of ITTE were not as prevalent as perhaps the TTA would have wished by the end of the 1990s and that a more realistic model could now be described as 'HEI-led':

> 'The motivation for the higher education-led model may either be pragmatic or prin-cipled. Course leaders may in principle be committed to the idea of collaboration but find insufficient schools willing to take on this degree of responsibility or they may have insufficient resources to support the degree of liaison necessary to develop a collabora-tive approach' Furlong et al., 2000, p. 117).

Furlong et al (ibid.) describe the idealised features of their 'HEI-led model' of partnership. One of these features relates to the assessment of students. They suggest that within this model assessment remains 'HEI-led and defined'.

The 'ideal' partnership arrangement is where students, provider-based personnel, school-based personnel and other partnership personnel (including, say, those from LEAs or diocese) are all equally involved in determining assessment procedures, the assessment of the students against the Standards and evaluation of the success of procedures. All this relies on a corporate understanding of the role and purpose of partnership in ITTE which is shared and equally valued by all the partners referred to above.

Determinants of 'ideal' models

The key determinants of the 'ideal' partnership model could be said to include:

- the mechanism by which schools and settings are recruited to a specific provider's partnership in the first place;
- the mechanism by which school-based personnel (mentors) are trained on first coming into partnership;
- the mechanism by which regular 'update' training is provided for mentors;
- the involvement of staff from all areas of the partnership in the training of each other; and
- the arrangements for transference of resource to remunerate partners for their involvement.

The first of these points is fundamentally important. If a school's initial recruitment is to satisfy a provider's emergency need to place students rather than as a part of managed growth of the partnership, it is likely that mentor training needs will follow demand on the ground. In the early stages of the relationship, students might end up being assessed by school-based personnel who themselves are not fully trained in the assessment procedures of the partnership.

The diversity of the mentoring role is very great and it is essential that mentors are rigorously trained in the one part of the role that might actually determine a student's ultimate achievement of QTS itself. Field describes mentoring as being 'a combination of being a "friend", "counsellor", "supporter", "a shoulder to cry on", "assessor", "facilitator", "advisor", and "role model"'. Unless mentors are introduced to the role of assessor carefully and through progressive mentor training, they are likely to let others of Field's 'roles' push the one of assessor to the back.

There is some variation from provider to provider as to who trains mentors, who has the overview responsibility for mentor training, how often 'update' training takes place, and how involved school-based personnel are in being trainers themselves. Assessment of students in school and within the HEI might, in the most developed of partnerships, be carried out at either the school or a provider base by personnel from either the school or the provider. Similarly, training of school and provider-based assessors might, and should, take place in either type of venue and be led by personnel from either type of venue.

Central to the success of mentor assessment of students is the degree to which mentors see themselves as objective assessors. Communication between student and school-based assessor becomes critical:

> *'If the student is to gain insights from the experienced teacher, the student needs to have the skill to elicit that information, and the teacher needs to offer the student such opportunities'* (Mills, 1998, p. 129).

The analogy of the student being the 'guest bearing gifts' and the mentor acting as the 'host' (Edwards, 1997) has to be overcome. Mills (1998, p. 130) goes further arguing that the real issue is self-awareness by both learner and assessor of their own 'competencies':

> 'Once we become an expert in the classroom, we become unconsciously competent, and often unaware of the implicit knowledge which ensures our success. The students, however, are initially often unconsciously incompetent, in that they do not have the understanding to know what they need to do or say. There seems therefore a need for the teachers to be conscious of their competence in order to make it explicit and therefore access the students to the skills, knowledge and understanding they possess thereby making them initially conscious of their incompetence.'

The final point concerns the way that a partnership school or setting is remunerated for its involvement. Remuneration policy varies enormously from provider to provider. Arguably, one extreme is represented by the G/RTP where a school is directly rewarded by the TTA for its involvement in ITTE. SCITTs represent another approach to funding schools' involvement in ITTE as the schools themselves are providing the ITTE route.

For larger HEI providers who may have partnerships that run into hundreds of different schools across several LEAs, there are a number of issues surrounding remuneration. Perhaps the fundamental question here, though, is what does the partnership do to ensure that there are developmental benefits to all parties within it?

Beneath all this lies the need to have a rigorous system for ensuring that HEI and school-based assessors are acquainted with the Standards and are kept informed as assessment practice changes when, for example, the Standards are revised. Assessors need to understand the reason for each specific assessment approach and why specific assignments are set. Where a student might evidence progress towards, or achievement of, a specific Standard it is essential the assessor understands the need for reliability and consistency in assessment practice.

Training and preparation of ITTE assessors

All personnel involved in the assessment of ITTE students need to be trained in assessment practices including the ways that the partnership moderates assessment of students. The code of practice suggests a number of ways by which providers might ensure that staff are following good practice.

From institution to institution there is great variation as to who is assessing students and how assessors are deployed. The following are some of the obvious variants:

- models of partnership employed (from 'full mentoring' to 'supervision' by provider);
- the number of 'observations' of lessons that might be made, their duration and resultant feedback;
- the degree to which a provider employs associate (part-time) tutors;
- the degree to which providers utilise non-school settings in which students might evidence the Standards;

- the degree to which students are involved in self-assessment;
- the degree to which assessment is carried out through practical projects other than assessed class teaching or paper assignments;
- the degree to which open and distance learning and information and communication technology (ICT)-related approaches are utilised in assessment; and
- the degree to which professional studies curriculum and education assignments are linked to practical planning, teaching and assessment in school.

The variation in how a student is 'handled' when they are assessed is very great. In school students can feel, on the one hand, that they are assessed at specifically defined assessment points (e.g. a prearranged lesson observation by a mentor) or, on the other, in a more developmental way via 'active mentoring' whereby a mentor provides ongoing feedback as he or she spends time with a student who is teaching (Collison, 1998).

The training and preparation regime for those who assess student teachers needs to be carefully determined and adhered to if quality is to be assured. The code of practice lists the major considerations as ensuring that assessors:

- gain access to and learn about new approaches to assessment and their implementation;
- receive induction when they are new to an assessment responsibility;
- know, and effectively and consistently use, a partnership's assessment strategies;
- are trained in using the Standards and the handbook;
- can report consistently and objectively against the Standards;
- receive preparation in observing and assessing against the Standards;

and that

- external examiners/external assessors are fully conversant with the Standards and the evidence required against them.

The degree of variation between providers as to how they train their own staff in new approaches to assessment is difficult to ascertain. Colleagues in different institutions point to their ongoing staff-development procedures but are often unwilling to go much further. Practice in this regard is probably most explicitly described when HEIs or other providers have colleagues whose role is specifically 'teaching and learning' development. Institutions point to their 'teaching and learning fellows' or similar designated appointments and emphasise specific work that such colleagues have done to advance assessment practice among their teaching teams.

Approaches to inducting new colleagues vary in their success. Central to the problem is the variety of colleagues who can come new to assessment within higher education.

Ensuring adequate training and preparation of all staff involved in partnership should have its root in provider-based and school-based staff being trained alongside each other. Providers report greatly varying practice in this respect, with many leaving mentor training to a small number of provider-based staff who have carved it out as a 'niche' in their work. Certainly training and preparation that focus specifically on assessing to the Standards seem to be most effective when colleagues from school and provider work together. Some of the best practice is reported to be when clustering of schools involves link tutors from the provider and leading mentors who take a co-ordinating role.

Supporting ITTE students in their progress towards and achievement of the Standards

The code of practice encourages providers to consider the guidance they give students on:

- their progress against the Standards, their strengths and further development needs, resultant action to be taken, support required and who should provide such support;
- how to use the Standards and the handbook as a focus for their training and development;
- using assessment outcomes to address weaknesses and to target set;
- reviewing their performance and constructing portfolios of evidence against the Standards; and
- how final assessment against the Standards will be conducted and how the results will be shared with the student.

Perhaps the main variants here are as follows:

- When are the Standards first introduced to the student?
- What recording system is used for logging successful evidencing?
- How is evidence collected, collated and presented?
- The mechanism by which students manage their own progress through the Standards.
- How are students provided with regular reviews and target-setting opportunities?
- Who has the authority to ratify successful evidencing?

On the first of these there is still some considerable variation. On PGCE courses the Standards are introduced immediately simply because of the time available within the course. On three or four-year undergraduate courses there is more variation. Some providers introduce the Standards very early on so that students can get used to what they are and what their purpose is. The notion of formative assessment and 'progress towards' is supported by this approach. Some providers even ratify certain specific Standards as having been evidenced within the first year of a degree course. PGCE flexible (modular) route students and G/RTP students may be able to demonstrate evidence of some Standards at the point of the Individual Needs Assessment.

Some undergraduate route providers record evidencing of the Standards in two (or three) 'waves'. It is certainly common for providers to encourage students to aim at evidencing certain Standards by the completion of their penultimate block experience, and then to evidence the bulk of the rest during their final block.

There is a considerable range of models as to how students gather evidence, record it and manage their own progress through the Standards. Following the publication of Circulars 10/97 and 4/98 (DfEE, 1997; 1998b) there were various warnings of the challenges that lay ahead for course designers in avoiding a movement to 'checklists' (Hogbin and Jarmany, 1998). Providers seem to agree on the notion that the gathering of evidence is the student's responsibility but that such evidence is carefully recorded is made particularly important by OFSTED's need to have a clear understanding of specific students' progress when ITTE is inspected.

A profile document in which assessment evidence is logged against groups of Standards is now commonplace among providers. Students note where the evidence can be found. For example:

- 'mentor's report – third-year Block Experience';
- 'written feedback after seminar on reporting to parents'; or
- 'feedback on ICT assignment in semester 4'.

They then sign and date against the evidence record. Ratification is then required from a seminar tutor or mentor in school and, slowly, the record of achievement is completed.

The concern that many providers have about signing against a Standard as having been evidenced early in a course is that the Standards are criterion-referenced and summative at the point of final achievement. They are meant to evidence a 'levelness' of work that reflects the student who is ready to be awarded QTS and therefore is moving towards the completion of his or her period of study.

Providers vary in the degree to which they identify progress in working towards Standards, set targets based on regularly measured progress and, then, ultimately, record the final realisation of the Standards. More than one provider defends the fact that they delay introduction and completion of the Standards until towards the end of the course on the basis that they don't want students' earlier assessment experiences to be overly governed by the Standards.

Documentation and recording of the assessment of students against the Standards

Providers broadly seem to agree on the documentary evidence that can combine to evidence the Standards. The code of practice suggests that the following are some of the sources from which evidence of the Standards might ultimately be drawn:

- subject audit tests;
- directed study tasks and assignments;
- classroom observations (lesson plans, tutors' comments and trainee's evaluations);
- evidence of planning and teaching to clear objectives;
- reviews with the student showing specific evidencing of Standards;
- personal targets against the Standards and evidence of their achievement;
- materials/resources prepared by the trainee and pupils' work;

- trainee's recording and monitoring evidence, setting of pupil targets and contribution to reports;
- reports demonstrating class organisation and managed pupil behaviour; and
- successful completion of the QTS skills tests.

Most providers use all the above approaches to provide sources of evidence for students in evidencing the Standards. There is little variety with respect to the use of audits tests in the subjects although some minor difference as to when they are first administered and then how the record of audits being passed is then used to evidence Standards. There has been a lessening of the setting of directed tasks and assignments in the non-core National Curriculum subjects, and certainly the tasks that are used are now very closely related to the Standards in way they weren't even recently.

All providers have gone to some effort to restructure lesson observation form and feedback sheets to students so that they are based around Standards groupings. The best practice seems to involve the lesson observation form being designed to lead the observer into focusing on Standards groupings and then mentor and college moderator or supervisor reports at the end of school blocks being written to the same system. Such reports are then a very workable evidence source for students as they go to mentors and college tutors asking for them to ratify Standards as having been achieved.

Most providers have a system where regular reviews are based on a Standards profile document. The design of this document varies quite markedly. Apart from anything else, different providers will have grouped the Standards in slightly different ways. A common approach seems to be for the document to contain a column for students to record the sourcing of their evidence against each specific standard (each row relating to each Standard) and then a column for a mentor or tutor to initial and date that he or she confirms that he or she has seen the evidence. The document is brought to the mentor at the end of a school block or to the seminar tutor at regular review meetings for confirmation signatures.

Ultimately a student will amass their Standards profile document, similar documents evidencing achievement of the Standards in the subjects, subject audits and QTS skills test certificates and then be in a position to seek final agreement that they have achieved all the Standards, enabling them to be recommended for QTS. There is variation as to how this collection of material is collated and presented by the student. Many providers suggest that its 'rightful home' is along with the student's portfolio of evidence which is itself often an assessed document.

External examining of programmes which include the assessment of students against the Standards.

The code of practice sets out in some detail how external examining can help ensure rigour and quality within and between providers. The code reflects on the need for examiners to be of the right expertise, with appropriate levels of professional experience, specifically in assessing to the Standards. It also makes the point that providers must have the right procedures with respect to clearly determining roles, powers and responsibilities and using external examiners' reports to modify practices as a part of quality assurance.

Brown *et al.* (1997, p. 246) suggest that the *'two main tasks of external examiners are to protect students and to safeguard standards'*. 'Safeguarding standards' is beginning to include a role for the external examiner as confirmer of satisfactory evidencing of the Standards. There is great variation, however, as to the degree to which external examiners have a say in confirming the final, synoptic stage.

It is certainly the case that different approaches exist as to how external assessors are used with respect to confirming students' evidencing of the Standards and commenting on providers' structures, systems and procedures in assessing students against the Standards. Variation certainly exists from a theoretical 'ideal' where an external opinion would be sought at the validation stage of a programme and throughout its active 'life'. External opinion should be sought on all assignment titles and then copies of all relevant course documentation made available to external examiners prior to the assessment period along with contextual course documentation. If all this is done as standard practice, an external examiner should be in a good position to provide comment on whether evidence used against Standards is viable, appropriate and substantiated. In addition to this, it is important that a sample of students is seen in school by external assessors who are from a provider background and who are used to assessing students to the Standards. Such cross-institution moderation is important if a provider is going to be able to demonstrate that its decisions on students' evidencing of the Standards in the school setting are appropriate and levelled to the sector in general. Some providers may have some way to go in developing the most rigorous of practices in these quality assurance areas. Selection and deployment of external examiners who understand the Standards, and can corroborate student performance in the light of them, are an important issue that has been taken only partially seriously by some providers. Many providers remember the warning contained in the Green Paper, *Teachers: Meeting the Challenge of Change* (DfEE, 1998a, p. 44), that *'one option would be for the Teacher Training Agency to accredit all external examiners of initial teacher training courses'*.

Conclusion

The code of practice sets out to *'support providers in their development, design and use of assessment strategies which are accurate, reliable and consistent'* (TTA, 2001). The code is a useful 'checklist' against which providers should audit their assessment systems.

In examining the code and using it as a framework for considering assessment practice in ITTE following Circular 4/98 and with the introduction of the revised Standards and ITTE requirements in January 2002, it becomes clear that providers of different types and of different sizes are operating a varied practice. Changing ITTE assessment practice in the light of the enormous impact of the Standards has varied from one provider to the next. The desire to hold on to what has worked well at the institution level has been immense, but the pressure to perform well when under OFSTED scrutiny has inevitably resulted in providers looking carefully at each other and adopting TTA/OFSTED 'friendly' practice when it is seen to work elsewhere.

The pace of change has resulted in providers developing their assessment practice very quickly, often without the opportunity to do so in a reflective way that involves national or at least regional consensus in approaches. A range of providers have all worked often quite independently to develop their assessment practice in the light of the Standards and have, in many respects (for example, Standards profile documentation), ended up with similar solutions.

The revised Standards are now simpler in the way they are set out and are clearer to interpret and an opportunity exists for providers to further clarify their assessment procedures to the ultimate benefit of the student teacher.

References

Brown, G., Bull, J. and Pendlebury, M. (1997) *Assessing Student Learning in Higher Education*. London: Routledge.

Collison, J. (1998) 'Mentoring – realising the true potential of school-based ITE.' In C. Richards, *et al.* (eds.) *Primary Teacher Education. High Status? High Standards?* London: Falmer, pp. 173–80.

Department for Education and Employment (DfEE) (1997) *Teaching: High Status, High Standards*. Circular 10/97. London: DfEE.

DfEE (1998a) *Teachers: Meeting the Challenge of Change*. Green Paper. London: HMSO.

DfEE (1998b) *Teaching: High Status, High Standards*. Circular 4/98. London: DfEE.

Department for Education and Skills (DfES) and Teacher Training Agency (TTA) (2002) *Qualifying to Teach: Professional Standards for Qualified Teacher Status and Requirements for Initial Teacher Training*. London: DfES/TTA..

Edwards, A. (1997) Guests bearing gifts: the position of student teachers in primary school classrooms. *British Educational Research Journal* 23(1).

Field, K. (1997) You and your mentor. *Mentoring and Tutoring* 4(3).

Furlong, J., Barton, L., Miles, S., Whiting, C. and Whitty, G. (2000) *Teacher Education in Transition: Reforming Professionalism*. Buckingham: Open University Press.

Hogbin, J. and Jarmany, K. (1998) Circular 10/97: implications for course design and development. In C. Richards *et al.* (eds.) *Primary Teacher Education. High Status? High Standards?* London: Falmer, pp. 36–45

Hyland, R. and Jacques, K. (2000) The complete teacher. In K. Jacques and R. Hyland (eds.) *Achieving QTS. Professional Studies: Primary Phase*. Exeter: Learning Matters.

Mills, K. (1998) Towards effective communication. In C. Richards *et al.* (eds.) *Primary Teacher Education. High Status? High Standards?* London: Falmer, pp. 128–36.

Office for Standards in Education (OFSTED) (1999) *Primary Follow-up Survey of the Training of Trainee Teachers to Teach Number and Reading, 1996–98*. London: OFSTED.

Sixsmith, C. (1998) Mentor assessment of trainee competence – the introduction of grading. In C. Richards *et al.* (eds.) *Primary Teacher Education. High Status? High Standards?* London: Falmer, pp. 181–89.

Teacher Training Agency (TTA) (2001) *Handbook to Accompany the Standards for the Award of Qualified Teacher Status and Requirements for the Provision of Initial Teacher Training* (consultation document). London: TTA.

Chapter 8: Subject specialism: here today, gone tomorrow?
Mark Whitfield and Sandra Eady

The debate surrounding the importance of subject knowledge for teaching has gathered momentum through research and the development of government policy for many years, but particularly in the last decade. The Department for Education and Employment (DfEE) Circular 4/98 (DfEE, 1998) has reinforced the role of the specialist subject by making it a requirement of all initial teacher training and education (ITTE) courses to prepare the teachers to teach at least one specialist subject. The new revised Standards for ITTE (DfES, 2002) have removed this requirement and this appears to indicate a change of thinking in regard to subject specialism being an essential element in primary ITTE. However, whilst the new document states that the new requirements for subject and age phase represent the minimum it also suggests that:

> 'many primary teacher trainers will choose to supplement this by continuing to offer a subject or phase specialism. Other trainers may choose to provide additional training which develops trainee teachers' knowledge and skills' (ibid., p. 3).

This chapter will consider the kind of teacher that will emerge from the new Standards. It will consider interpretations of teachers' subject knowledge arising from research and relate and compare this to the definition that emerges from Circular 4/98 (DfEE, 1998) and the revised regulations (DfES/TTA, 2002). The chapter will evaluate a selection of current undergraduate and postgraduate ITTE programmes based on the 4/98 Standards and consider possible revisions necessary in order to meet the new requirements. The chapter will attempt to describe the new kind of teacher that is likely to emerge from the new Standards.

Concerns relating to subject knowledge are not new and in fact were apparent in Her Majesty's Inspectors' (HMI) surveys of Newly Qualified Teachers (NQTs) where many were judged to have an inadequate grasp of subject knowledge and a limited idea about making specific the aims of a lesson and the marking of work to inform assessment and future planning (HMI, 1988). Bennett and Carre (1993) argue that the findings from their research point strongly to the importance of teachers' subject knowledge in relation to effective teaching. This raises such questions as 'how can teachers teach well knowledge they do not fully understand?' Bennett and Carre go on to suggest, 'student teachers with specialist knowledge are more likely to stress conceptual understanding and syntactic knowledge, whereas non-specialists simply taught the content.' Thus they conclude: 'content knowledge affects both what teachers teach and how they teach it. Depth of knowledge also appears to influence pedagogical choices' (ibid., p. 9). Whilst this research refers to teaching in secondary schools there was growing concern that similar issues were becoming apparent in primary schools.

A key influence on Bennett and Carre's work has been the influential research of Shulman (1987) and Grossman et al. (in Reynolds, 1989) on knowledge bases for teaching. Shulman's work has involved the development of clear categories relating to different kinds of knowledge required for teaching. In sum, these are;

- content knowledge;
- general pedagogical knowledge;
- curriculum knowledge;
- pedagogical-content knowledge;
- knowledge of learners and their characteristics; and
- knowledge of educational contexts.

One of the most recent considerations of the importance of knowledge bases for the student teacher in relation to initial teacher training has arisen from the research of Turner-Bisset (1999). She has added to Shulman's seven knowledge bases and argues that the model of knowledge essential for initial teacher training presented by Circular 10/97 (DfEE, 1997) requirements is inadequate, presenting only part of the picture.

Turner-Bisset (1999) suggests that pedagogical content knowledge, knowledge required in relation to the transferring of pure subject knowledge for teaching, is *'the set which contains all other sets* (ibid, p. 47).' In other words, pedagogical content knowledge consists of a range of other knowledge bases on which a teacher draws upon in order to teach. Turner-Bisset suggests that trainee teachers draw on some of these knowledge bases, whereas effective (and usually more experienced teachers) make use of the range of knowledge bases.

Alexander *et al.* (1992) recognised the value of the specialist in the primary classroom and the importance of having subject experts to provide important leadership and academic rigour in the primary context. They reinforced the importance of sound subject knowledge and viewed subject knowledge as a central theme in the raising of standards in teaching and learning. Paragraph 133 states that *'Classroom practice will improve if it is grounded in knowledge and understanding of the subject matter to be taught'* (ibid., p. 37). Whilst it is realised that it is not possible for primary teachers to have a high level of subject knowledge in all National Curriculum areas this document is very clear about the important role increased and specialised subject knowledge can play in raising standards in the primary classroom. The implication is that all primary school teachers and not just subject co-ordinators need an increased subject knowledge if they are to be effective in moving children on in their learning. Thus it was not surprising to see that developing a subject specialism during initial teacher training was a significant aspect of the 4/98 Standards.

Alexander *et al.* (1992, p. 44) also suggest that there is a requirement to balance the *'pupil's need for security and stability with their need to follow a curriculum which, because it is rooted in secure subject knowledge, is challenging and stimulating'*. On this basis they advocate a variety of possible roles a primary teacher may take on, namely, the generalist, the generalist/consultant, the semi-specialist and the specialist (ibid., p. 43).

The report suggests that the specialist teacher has a number of roles. Primarily the specialist supports other colleagues. They also suggest that the specialist manages curriculum and resources and teaching specialist lessons. Specialists are expected to raise the standard within the subject through influencing whole-school development and planning. It is perhaps not difficult to understand why Circular 4/98 (DfEE, 1998) mirrors the underlying themes developed through research, policy and the National Curriculum: the development of sound subject knowledge and specialist subject knowledge for at least one curriculum subject at a higher level should be a key element of ITTE.

Whilst 'pure' subject knowledge was a key factor in determining the nature of Circular 4/98, there is also evidence that other aspects of teaching and learning were considered equally important. Shulman's model suggests that the practitioner first engages with the content knowledge of a given subject and that once this is grasped it must be translated or modified in a way that is understandable and comprehensible to pupils. In order to do this the practitioner has to prepare the most appropriate materials and resources, consider how the key idea might be best explained through analogy, what teaching approach is most suitable, as well as develop the skill to differentiate to suit the needs of the pupils. All this has to be done, he argues, within the context of classroom management and organisation.

It could be argued that in order to prepare the teacher effectively, the Standards for the award of Qualified Teacher Status (QTS) should engage the student with each of these knowledge bases. *Qualifying to Teach* (DfES/TTA, 2002) appears to have changed the emphasis of ITTE, moving away from the notion of the specialist and towards the professional and pedagogical. Although it doesn't seem to address directly the idea of gradually mastering a skill in order to meet a Standard, it could be argued that it provides more opportunity to develop the notion of Shulman's (1987) seven knowledge bases for the trainee teacher, by seemingly freeing up space in teacher training for providers to reinterpret the notion of specialism in the primary school.

The new Standards reinforce the view that ITTE is very much the first step in training and qualification. Described in the Foreword as the start of a long-term process of professional development, there seems to be a widening view of what knowledge is and a broadening of the concept of the specialist, particularly in relation to the primary school teacher. The Foreword states: *'the standards will ensure that all new teachers have the subject knowledge and the teaching and learning expertise they need'* (DfES/TTA, 2002, p. 1). However, in the Introduction it goes on to say that teaching demands *'knowledge and practical skills,'* (ibid., p. 2) without clarifying what is meant by knowledge. In the new Standards professional values and practice are to the fore. In terms of knowledge and understanding trainees are expected to be 'confident and authoritative' in the subjects they teach. This seems to be quite a significant difference in comparison to the present Standards as there is no reference to specialist teachers or experts.

Whereas it clearly defines secure knowledge and understanding in secondary training as equivalent to degree level, there is no clear definition for what a secure knowledge and understanding might mean at primary level. The 4/98 Standards are quite clear and prescriptive. Thus, whilst the definition of secure subject knowledge is left open to interpretation at primary level, it is clear by its very absence that there is now no requirement to develop specialist subject knowledge in any of the National Curriculum areas (which in the past has been deemed as 'A levelness') for primary ITTE.

In order to understand the implications of the new Standards in terms of subject teaching it is worth making a comparative study of aspects of the Knowledge and understanding sections in the old and the new Standards. *Qualifying to Teach* (DfES/TTA, 2002) is a less detailed document than its predecessor, leading to a narrowing of minimum requirements and broader interpretations of meaning. *Qualifying to Teach* (ibid., R. 2.1) states that to be awarded QTS the trainee must *'have a secure knowledge and understanding of the subject(s) they are trained to teach'*. Previously the trainee was expected to *'understand the purposes, scope, structure and balance of the National Curriculum Orders as a whole and, within them, the place and scope of the primary phase, the key stages, the primary core and foundation subjects; and RE'* (DfEE, 1998, p. 4) and be *'aware of the breadth of content covered by the pupils' National Curriculum across the primary core and foundation subjects and RE'* (ibid., p. 4). Trainees were also expected to have *'a detailed knowledge and understanding of the relevant National Curriculum programmes of study and level descriptions or end of key stage descriptions across the primary age range'* (ibid., p. 4). From a position where trainee teachers had to have a detailed understanding of the National Curriculum, the trainee qualifying under the new orders will not even need to have an understanding of, or the experience of teaching, all the National Curriculum subjects. *Qualifying to Teach* (DfES/TTA, 2002, p. 7) states that ITTE providers must ensure that trainees:

'have sufficient understanding of a range of work across the following subjects:

- *history or geography*
- *physical education*
- *ICT*
- *art and design or design and technology*
- *performing arts, and*
- *Religious Education.'*

and *'to be able to teach them in the age range for which they are trained, with advice from an experienced colleague where necessary'*. It is conceivable, should a provider choose, that a trainee may qualify having never been formally trained, educated or having taught one or more of a number of National Curriculum subjects, including history, geography, design and technology, art and music. Whilst Circular 4/98 stated that the trainee should *'for any non-core, non-specialist subject covered in their training, have a secure knowledge to a Standard equivalent to at least level 7 of the pupils' National Curriculum. For RE, the required standard for non-specialist training is broadly equivalent to the end of Key Stage statements for Key Stage 4 in QCA's Model Syllabuses for RE'* (DfEE, 1998, p. 4).

The new Standards make no requirement on the depth of specialist knowledge a trainee should possess; instead they have to demonstrate *'sufficient understanding across a range of work'* (DfES/TTA, 2002, p. 7).

The Office for Standards in Education (OFSTED) (2001, P. 3) suggests that *'there are some worrying features* [in course design] *which threaten the sustained provision of a pool of well-qualified subject specialists across the primary school curriculum, both at regional and national levels'*. It is ironic that on the one hand government bodies are warning about threats to the number of subject specialists in primary schools when other government agencies are removing the need for specialisms in Primary ITTE.

Despite the absence of the requirement to develop a subject specialism it is perhaps useful to recognise how the notion of developing subject knowledge in the broader sense in the new Standards fits with Shulman's (1987) seven knowledge bases discussed earlier. It could be argued that the new Standards encourage a broader development and definition of subject knowledge and specialist rather than the narrower, in-depth notion of subject specialism advocated by Circular 4/98.

The new model of teacher emerging from the revised Standards ensures that trainees have a secure grasp of the broad knowledge bases required for teaching. The development of subject specialism or specialism in a non-curriculum area appears not to be a priority but perhaps is an element of teaching that can begin in ITTE and develop in early and continuing professional development. In this sense, the revised Standards and emerging definition of the kind of teacher to be trained fit more comfortably within the longer-term vision of ITTE being the first step along the path of an evolving and dynamic teaching career. Whilst this seems to fit quite neatly with the current thinking it does beg the question as to why there appears to have been such a radical change in thinking. Documentation prior to and including the 4/98 Standards suggested a need for an emphasis on the development of subject knowledge for ITTE, particularly at primary level. Now the focus seems to have shifted more to developing 'professional values and practice.'

Perhaps such a change in governmental policy with regard to the Standards reflects the fact that the government has listened to teacher training institutions. Many have warned that it is impossible for all teachers in training to meet realistically the 4/98 Standards; to study one or more specialist subjects at the same time creates further stress and anxiety amongst students and that essentially there are far too many 'technical' Standards realistically to assess, thus preventing a focus on developing pedagogy and professionalism.

The new Standards do seem to be more manageable, more generic and realistic. The removal of specialism does free up time to focus more on pedagogy and building other aspects of a teacher's knowledge base. However the removal of specialism and the reduced emphasis on subject knowledge in favour of professional values and pedagogy perhaps deserve further discussion, particularly in relation to the kind of teacher that is likely to emerge from the new Standards.

Turner-Bisset (1999) may provide us with another explanation as to the change in policy for ITTE. She suggests that three elements (the importance of subject matter knowledge in teaching, the notion of partnership between schools and higher education institutes (HEIs) and the competency-based movement) have been brought together in the

Standards for teacher training. Thus it is reasonable to assume that this underlying rationale for teacher training Standards, along with the government's theme of account-ability and value for money, has led to the move towards rethinking the Standards so that more training can take place in schools. The removal of subject specialism and a greater focus on professional values and teaching would make this even more feasible within the school context.

Whilst HEIs (and many primary schools) questioned the prospect of subject specialism being developed effectively and adequately through school-based training, there did not seem to be a feeling that it should be removed from the training requirements altogether. The concerns raised by schools and HEIs was confirmed in *Subject Specialist Courses in Primary Initial Teacher Training* (OFSTED, 2001) where school-based training, in relation to subject specialism, was judged as *'less good and commonly insufficiently subject focused'* (ibid., p. 2).

The link between subject content knowledge and pedagogic content knowledge, particularly in relation to specialism was, and still is, felt to be a crucial aspect of becoming an effective teacher and thus a central part to teacher training, not just in secondary, but also in primary schools. Thus the elimination of this requirement from the new Standards must raise suspicion that there may be another reason for doing this. By removing the specialism requirement from the Standards for ITTE, it allows school-based routes to meet more easily the Standards for teacher training. In fact it could be argued that they appear to be better placed in providing more effective and relevant 'on the job' training now that greater status seems to have been given to some Standards, namely professional values and practice; new Standards could be seen as to favour and to make more attractive school-based routes into teaching. Thus, instead of improving the quality of ITTE, the new Standards, by removing the requirement of subject specialism, are really addressing the supply and recruitment issue of teacher shortage.

Initial teacher educators will be required to change their provision to reflect the new Standards. Undergraduate courses will need to provide the balance between the minimalist nature of the new Standards and the need to maintain degree worthiness. There is an expectation that courses will continue to offer some of the breadth and depth of current provision, and changes to provision should be justified professionally and decisions about changes to course content should be made after extensive consul-tation with partnership schools. To change the nature of provision for purely financial or resourcing reasons would be a mistake. New models will need to take into account professional needs and skills in teaching before developing specific expertise in a specialism. New course outlines must also regard specialism in a broader context than the more traditional curriculum subjects, which reiterates Shulman's research relating to knowledge bases.

How might courses change to reflect the new Standards? Which route into teaching benefits most from the changes in requirements? In order to address these questions we will consider three key routes into primary teaching: the traditional four-year undergraduate degree, the three-year undergraduate route and the increasingly popular Professional Certificate in Education (PGCE).

Route 1

Currently, on a typical four-year undergraduate degree, 30–35% of the degree is made up of a specialist subject. The specialist subjects are often in traditional curriculum subjects (see Figure 8.1). Under the new Standards one might expect the specialist subjects to be more diverse in nature, reflecting the suggestion within *Qualifying to Teach* (DfES/TTA, 2002, p. 3) that initial teacher educators may choose to offer *'a specialist area of study such as the teaching of children with special education needs, or gifted and more able pupils, or a curriculum area such as Personal, Social and Health Education and Citizenship'* or *'a non-National Curriculum subject specialism'*.

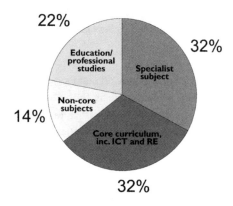

Figure 8.1 A typical four-year programme

It may be beneficial to develop a four-year undergraduate route that allows the trainee to qualify with QTS after three years and then offer a fourth year to develop a specialism which contributes towards a post-graduate qualification (see Table 8.1).

Table 8.1 Route 1, version 1

Year 1	Year 2	Year 3	Year 4	Year 5	Year 6
Three-year degree in primary education			One-year specialism	NQT year	Year two
BA (Hons) in primary education with QTS			½ MA/ Med	½ MA/ Med (distance learning)	

There may be opportunity to offer a four-year programme that is studied over five years and incorporates the NQT induction year (see Table 8.2).

Whilst the introduction of financial incentives for postgraduate recruits impacts on recruitment to four-year routes, the long-term future of the four-year undergraduate route will depend upon innovative programmes that offer unique opportunities to trainee teachers.

Table 8.2 Route 1, verson 2

Year 1	Year 2	Year 3	NQT year	Year 4	Year 6
Three-year degree in primary education			Induction year	One-year specialism	Year two
BA (Hons) in primary education with QTS			MA/Med (1-year full-time/2-year distance learning)		

Route 2

The three-year degree may be considered as the main undergraduate route into teaching – to qualify for the profession in three years has been a major incentive. A typical three-year undergraduate degree with a specialism contains 20–25% of subject specialism and these modules may, or may not, have a primary curriculum focus. It is conceivable that new courses may tend more towards offering specialist modules which more closely reflect classroom practice (see Figure 8.2).

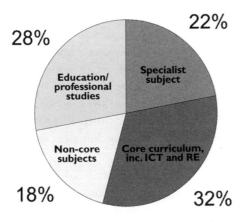

Figure 8.2 A typical three-year programme

It is conceivable that providers of three-year routes may widen the choice of specialism into non-subject, professional areas; it is also conceivable that providers may reduce, or possibly remove, the contribution of the specialism and increase the education/professional modules or modules which focus on general curriculum management. OFSTED (2001) states that 20% of routes into teaching do not have a specialism, and that this figure, especially in postgraduate routes, is likely to rise.

Possible non-National Curriculum specialisms could include:

- advanced studies in early years;
- special educational needs;
- multicultural education;

- citizenship;
- personal social health education;
- leadership and management;
- English as an additional language;
- more able/gifted pupils;
- education psychology; and
- modern foreign languages.

These changes would follow the guidance offered in the new Standards, reflect their generalist nature and reflect the position that ITTE is the first step of a teacher's professional development.

Route 3

Over the past five years there has been a proliferation of postgraduate and school-based routes into the teaching profession. These routes developed from a need to address the shortage of trainees entering the profession and, from a government perspective, are also financially better value for money. There are now full-time, part-time and modular courses and flexible learning routes managed so as to respond to the needs of the individual trainee. School-based courses (SCITTs) have become an important area of growth in ITTE.

Typically, the professional-graduate route will concentrate on professional/education studies and on the core curriculum. At present, there is less emphasis on the specialism as, traditionally, the trainee already has a degree in a curriculum subject (see Figure 8.3). Full-time professional-graduate programmes are likely to continue to place the emphasis on core curriculum and if specialisms are offered then they will reflect the broader perspective, beyond the traditional National Curriculum areas.

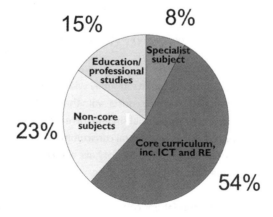

Figure 8.3 A typical full-time PGCE programme

It is within professional-graduate routes where the new Standards may have their greatest impact. The minimalist nature of the new Standards will lead to more trainees meeting the Standards more easily, especially on modular, trainee-focused, routes. This may address more quickly teacher shortages but it will be imperative that trainers ensure quality amongst their trainees. Early and continuing professional development will be essential if these new teachers are to remain in the profession.

The new Standards have removed the need to have a first degree in a curriculum subject; this is likely to broaden the appeal of the PGCE as those who haven't considered teaching may now feel able to pursue teaching as a career. The nature of PGCE courses must also address the needs of this new group of trainees.

The kind of teacher that will emerge from the new Standards could reflect the wider interpretation of 'specialism' given by the revised Standards. On the other hand, the new teacher emerging could be equipped with only the basic technical skills to operate in the classroom. The new Standards will allow providers to develop and enhance their courses reinterpreting the notion of specialism to reflect their view of the subject knowledge needed for teaching as well as the needs of the locality. Although this may allow for more creativity in developing teachers' subject knowledge within courses, it is likely to have financial implications in terms of the length of time it may take to qualify.

However, there is also now the possibility for a range of school-based courses to emerge which may just aim to meet the minimum requirements set down by the new Standards. In some ways these courses could become more attractive, financially and academically, to some trainee teachers who may prefer to acquire basic technical skills in order to get a teaching job quickly. There is a danger that if providers do refocus initial teacher training programmes just to meet the minimum requirements, it could reduce the status of ITTE to simply an accumulation of technical skills and reduce the status of subject knowledge. Although this may be a 'quick fix' to the problem of teacher recruitment threatening the quality of education at present, it must be ensured that such routes do not compromise the quality of ITTE and, in particular, the notion of subject knowledge/specialism by ensuring that they have strong links and obligations to accreditation to continuing professional development.

Providers of ITTE have a responsibility to develop provision that maintains standards of practice in the primary context. Whether subject specialism will be 'gone tomorrow' may depend on providers developing relevant courses which recognise the changing nature of primary specialisms.

References

Alexander, R., Rose, J. and Woodhead, C. (1992) *Curriculum Organisation and Classroom Practice in Primary Schools – a Discussion Paper*. London: HMSO.

Bennett, N. and Carre, C. (eds.) (1993) *Learning to Teach*. London: Routledge.

Department for Education and Employment (DfEE) (1997) *Teaching: High Status, High Standards*. Circular 10/97. London: DfEE.

DfEE (1998) *Teaching: High Status, High Standards. Requirements for Courses of Initial Teacher Training*. Circular 4/98. London: DfEE.

Department for Education and Skills (DfES) and Teacher Training Agency (TTA) (2002) *Qualifying to Teach: Professional Standards for Qualified Teacher Status and Requirements of Initial Teacher Training.* London: DfES/TTA.

Her Majesty's Inspectors (HMI) (1988) *The New Teacher in School. Survey by HM Inspectors in England and Wales.* London: HMSO.

Office for Standards in Education (OFSTED) (2001) *Subject Specialist Courses in Primary Initial Teacher Training.* London: OFSTED.

Reynolds, M. C. (1989) *The Knowledge Base of the Beginning Teacher.* Oxford: Pergamon.

Shulman, L. (1987) Knowledge and teaching: foundations of the new reform. *Harvard Educational Review* 57(1): 1–22.

Turner-Bisset, R. (1999) The knowledge bases of the expert teacher. *British Educational Research Journal* 25(1): 39-54.

Section 3:
Initial teacher training and education: a vision for the future

Initial teacher training and education (ITTE) has been the subject of constant change and development as the needs and aspirations of society have evolved. This process of reform and remoulding has accelerated in recent years as education in general and ITTE in particular have been the subject of attention from politicians who, arguably, across the political spectrum, have sought to develop popular educational ideologies that may be distant from research and professional communities. Wilkin (1996, p. 175) summarises powerfully this notion and, whilst she writes of the early 1990s, her words have very clear resonance today.

> 'The government has engaged in deeper political and ideological penetration of training ... Members of HEIs [higher education institutes] have become increasingly outspoken in their condemnation of the encroaching politicisation of training and the threat to the quality of professional preparation that this is considered to generate.'

The main purpose of this chapter is to take a glimpse glimpse into the future, to develop a vision for ITTE for the year 2015. In developing such a vision it is possible to approach this in at least two ways. In the first instance, there is an approach which is largely fantasy – that is, a dreaming of dreams devoid of any real grounding in the current orthodoxy, based on one's own deeply held values and beliefs about education. Here there is a tacit assumption that the likelihood of this becoming reality is rather slim. A second approach is to start with analysis of the push and pull forces in society and education and use this as a grounding to develop a considered perspective about the possible future shape of ITTE. In broad terms we wish to adopt the second approach whilst recognising that to do this without implicit reference to one's own values and beliefs is probably almost impossible. We recognise therefore that the chapter is not entirely value-neutral!

We have structured our thinking according to five main sections. The first section contains a broad overview of some important contextual factors both in education and in society at large. Moving on from this we wish to assert that the national 'Teaching and Learning Research Programme' has the potential to act as a transformational agent in a reconceptualisation of teaching and learning. A third section is concerned with a vision for the school curriculum and pedagogy and related to this, we consider some of the characteristics of ITTE, and teacher education in general. Finally, we wish to pose some key questions that will need to be answered if the vision we outline is to bear any resemblance to reality in the middle part of the next decade. This is important as we recognise fully that in a chapter of this length we can only put forward a brief outline of a view. It will be up to others to pick this up and consider it further.

Education and society

Any grounded perspective on the future must, at least in part, be based on a consideration of the present and here it is clear that there are a great number of well understood forces which are impacting on society. For example, we live in a rapidly changing international context. Following the events of 11 September 2001, the vacuum that was created at the end of the cold war has been filled dramatically by the so-called war against terrorism. In the West our attention has been shifted from the perceived threat of communism to that of religious fundamentalism and the new terror of a 'hidden' enemy, of cells of terrorists rather than defined countries. Clearly the events of the latter part of 2001 have educational implications centred on issues such as the understanding of cultures, tolerance and global education. It is also true that the power of multinationals is now rivalling nation-states and their actions have global implications for economies and societies. In January 2002, the West witnessed the demise of Enron and saw at first hand the economic and social implications of this for millions of people. Meanwhile new technologies create a global context where there is, particularly for the 'rich' countries ever faster communication, more communication and global shrinkage. Environmental change particularly through global warming is a medium term reality and, whilst often less dramatic in the short term, may prove yet to be the biggest force for change in the world, once the West perceives the potential economic threats it brings. Whilst we wouldn't wish to overstate the case, we would suggest that in part international events have a bearing on the direction of education policy at national level.

At national level, currently the UK is hovering in between full integration with Europe and developing closer ties with the USA. The debate has been raging for many years, particularly since the advent of the Common Market, but appears to have been given new momentum by 11 September and also the advent of the single currency in Europe. The next ten years may well see key developments and resolutions in this area. A rapidly ageing population creates an impetus for change within public services, especially the Health Service, and creates more political power for older sections of society. The transport infrastructure is coming under strain as increasing levels of communication have led to a continuous rise in the number of people on the move. Public–private finance initiatives create a kind of postmodern funding regime for public services, removing the old certainties of public and private sectors.

All these issues raise key questions about the main goals of education in an advanced capitalist society like ours. We contend that there are at least four main goals of education that match the needs of society in the early part of the twenty-first century.

1. Economic productivity

Arguably, economic productivity has been the most important driver of educational reform since New Labour came into power in 1997. Indeed the blueprint for Labour's second term in office, *Schools; Building on Success*, states that:

'Education is a recognised priority, not just for Government, but also for society as a whole. It is seen not only as the key to developing equality of opportunity, but also to enabling the nation to prepare for the emergence of the new economy and its increased demands for skills and human capital' (DfES, 2001, p. 8).

Its premise therefore is that in order to remain competitive in global terms, and ensure the continuation of our standard of life and global political prowess, we must have a well educated (well trained?) workforce, particularly within the so-called basic skills in literacy, numeracy and information and communication technology (ICT). The most striking piece of evidence for this aim occurred when the Office for Standards in Education (OFSTED) published its review of international surveys of educational achievement (Reynolds and Farrell, 1996) and pointed to the Pacific Rim countries as societies which were both globally competitive and on certain measures achieving high educational standards. We could argue at length about the validity of this, but the important point here is that politicians had looked to the education systems of economically successful countries as a way to develop the education systems within the UK, particularly England.

Looking to the future, given the West's desire to protect its own global position, we see that the economic rationale for education will be sustained throughout the early part of the twenty-first century. The pace of technological and therefore economic change will mean a continued focus on a highly skilled workforce. However we also see other aims coming to the fore over the next decade, some of which may have been less prominent since the mid-1990s.

2. Political acumen

At national level, there is currently increasing and widespread concern about the apparent rejection of national democratic political processes by large numbers of people. The 2001 general election was characterised by low turnout, particularly amongst younger people. This is not to say that society is entering into a period of anarchy; rather, a circumstance of apathy where political participation in the formal sense is becoming less than apparent. There are, of course, many reasons why this circumstance is occurring, such as the emergence of issues-based politics, a media-fuelled perception that sleaze is at the heart of politics and apathy stemming from affluence. Whatever the reason or reasons for this situation, education, we consider will increasingly be seen as part of the solution. This is, of course, politically important since democratic well-being is fundamental to the stability of our society and the stability of our society is, in turn, fundamental to global competitiveness.

This agenda is reflected clearly in the revised National Curriculum published in 2000, where in secondary education citizenship became a formal part of that curriculum and at primary level it formed part of non-statutory guidelines alongside personal, social and health education. There is in short a strengthening focus on how the individual relates to society, and how that individual participates in democracy. The political importance of citizenship is highlighted in the introduction to *Curriculum 2000*, by the then Secretary of State, David Blunkett, and William Stubbs, Chair of the Qualifications and Curriculum Authority (QCA). They state:

> *'Education in citizenship and democracy will provide coherence in the way in which all pupils are helped to develop a full understanding of their roles and responsibilities as citizens in a modern democracy. It will play an important role, alongside other aspects of the curriculum and school life, in helping pupils to deal with difficult moral and social questions that arise in their lives and in society'* (QCA, 1999, p. 4).

3. Individual fulfilment.

We see that during the next decade there will be a re-emergence of individual fulfilment as a politically acceptable educational aim. We take individual fulfilment to mean a matching of the education system to the needs and aspirations of individuals in society. Underpinning this is a sense in which there is a tacit acceptance that the meeting of individual needs and wants is allied to the meeting of society's purposes, particularly economic strength. It is interesting, in this respect, to note Murphy and Liu's (1998) analysis of Taiwanese education. They suggest that at the very time when the West was trying to search within Pacific Rim countries for educational solutions to economic growth, Taiwanese education was undergoing reform to focus more closely on the development of the whole person and a shift from an academic-centred curriculum to a student-centred curriculum. We have to be very careful when making comparisons across systems and cultures, but the question comes to mind as to whether in the UK higher standards will in the end be achieved without close reference to the individual.

If over the next decade or so there is to be a refocusing on the individual then, in effect, we argue that there will be a need for the educational pendulum to swing not back but to another plane. There will be a need for a paradigm shift. We would argue that currently there is some evidence of the primary education pendulum swinging back to a less prescriptive mode, but that this does not amount to this paradigm shift. Between 1976 (Jim Callaghan's Ruskin House speech) and 2000 there was a very well documented period of enhanced centralised control in all areas of education which, arguably, marginalised the individual and upheld the whole notion of groups achieving predetermined standards. Post 2000, there has been some evidence of a marginal liberalisation of education, particularly primary education. The new Standards and requirements for ITTE give providers more autonomy in the design of courses leading to the award of Qualified Teacher Status (QTS). The OFSTED methodology in primary education has been given a lighter touch, and *Curriculum 2000* (DfEE/QCA, 1999), too, provides evidence of a looser educational framework. Additionally, the reform spotlight has shifted from primary to secondary with the advent of the Key Stage 3 strategy. However we would argue that hitherto this does not amount to an acknowledgement that the nurturing of the individual is consistent with the achievement of high performance across the education system. Reform has concentrated on the systemic, rather than the individual. By 2015 we would urge a far more explicit recognition of the potential of a policy that focused on the individual as a person as opposed to the mechanical achievement of national targets within set areas of the curriculum. Such a recognition would see personal fulfilment through the achievement of high, but not always measurable, educational standards, as compatible with achievement of economic aims.

4. Cultural recognition

In many ways, of course, these are not new issues in education. There has been a multitude of policy statements, research papers and changing practice in relation to this area over the last forty years and more. However in the first part of the twenty-first century it seems that enhanced focus will need to be given to this area. Society has been rapidly transformed and the new world order demands that children have an understanding and respect for cultural and religious difference. Given the rapid changes in the social and cultural make-up of society, we see that the importance of understanding, recognising and respecting cultural diversification will be enhanced. In short we see that education has a fundamentally important part to play in ensuring the ongoing cohesiveness and stability of society.

Taken together these four aims of education in 2015 serve to create a rationale for the development of both primary education and primary ITTE. We shall return to these two themes later in this chapter. What is clear is that education is to remain high on the agenda in an uncertain and unstable world. You can imagine President Kennedy (the UK's Prime Minister in 2015) making a keynote speech at the beginning of the Parliamentary session which has the following core statement:

> 'Learning, learning, learning … We will fight poverty with learning, prejudice with learning and conflict with learning. We build tolerance, peace, freedom, participation and fulfilment with learning too. It is the cornerstone of our society and the foundation of our future. I am therefore pleased to announce today that the Government is investing further in the development of a new wave of Professional Development Schools which will recognise the contribution of all education professionals to the one central goal of achieving economic success through recognising the achievements of all individual pupils in our schools.'

The role of research

We have asserted that the reforms within education in general and within ITTE in particular have been driven largely by political ideology. This has been true of the last twenty years or so and is typified by this quotation from the Modes of Teacher Education (MOTE) team. Referring to the 1980s, Furlong et al. (2000, p. 2) state: 'initial teacher education, during the 1980s, increasingly became a major site for ideological struggle between the government and others, especially those in higher education.' This observation could apply equally to the 1990s, both pre- and post-New Labour. In one sense the education research community has been part of ideological battles too. In 1999, James Tooley published his report, commissioned by OFSTED, which sought to berate the inaccessibility of much of educational research, so arguing that its impact on classroom practice in general and the Standards-driven agenda in particular must have been rather minimal.

Yet we argue that if educational reform is to have real, sustained impact then educational research must be at the centre of the agenda. Indeed our vision of 2015 is one where a reconceptualisation of policy is based on a reconceptualisation of teaching and learning that emerges from large-scale, semi-autonomous educational research. The quotation from 'President Kennedy' (speaking in 2015) uses the language of learning as the sound bite, rather than the language of driving up standards.

It follows that the rolling out of the national Teaching and Learning Research Programme (TLRP) is absolutely critical to the future of education in this country. It is an opportunity for a context to be developed whereby research informs policy. By 2015 it is our aspiration that the research agenda has a direct impact on the practical experience of millions of pupils and indeed thousands of student teachers and that this impact is at a political and strategic level, rather than at the level of piecemeal reform.

At the centre of a research agenda in education at the beginning of the twenty-first century there are then perhaps two key initiatives. In the first instance we have an aspiration that central to the development of the programme will be a reconceptualisation of teaching and learning which sees the person as at the centre. There needs to be an acknowledgement of the affective dimension to education and the reality of a multitude of different learning styles and intelligences. Secondly, we argue for the performance agenda to be balanced more evenly with an agenda focused on the development of the individual. The former implies a process of objective measurement against predetermined criteria, whilst the latter celebrates the potential of human beings in a learning environment if educators are able to take account of all elements of a person. Both are concerned at least partly with the economic well-being of society but reach this goal in very different ways.

It follows that the notion of lifelong learning will continue to have political and social currency in the early part of this century – and that life-wide learning may become equally important. Here we mean the process whereby a person's learning is seen much more holistically with educators taking an enhanced interest in a person's experience outside formal schooling. All this will mean a shift of interest such that the context for learning will be seen as a significant element in the achievement of high standards and ultimately competitive economic performance. The role of educational research, such as TLRP, will be very important in helping us to understand the importance of context and the complexity of pedagogy.

A vision of schooling in 2015

If we are to consider a vision for ITTE then we first need to consider the kind of primary education that is being seen as 'cutting edge' in 2015. In considering this we will, of course, be making certain assumptions about the political context of education by 2015. These are as follows.

1. There has been a paradigm shift in thinking about education at policy level. This involves a recognition that in order for the economic and social aspirations of society to be met there needs to be a focus on the individual and individual identity. This is clearly different from the paradigm of the late 1990s where the key to economic success was a driving up of standards based on a systems approach to education.

2. Educational research has influenced the development of policy in fundamental ways not seen in the 1990s. There is an assumption here that educational research has a degree of autonomy, that there is no hint of politically driven research and that research findings are interpreted by policy-makers such that there is a degree of cohesion between research and policy.

3. The goals of education are, in broad terms, four-fold, related to continued economic prosperity, personal fulfilment, the development of cultural integration and recognition and the development of political acumen.

4. The final three goals are each necessary but not sufficient conditions for the first goal to be met and there is in government and society a widespread if intuitive understanding of this.

5. The political climate is characterised by a listening culture whereby educators and researchers are engaged in a constructive and inclusive dialogue with government that is the fuel of real and sustainable change in education.

6. Public–private finance initiatives are a well developed and accepted part of society. By 2015 lessons have been learnt from earlier difficulties with this form of funding and a framework has been created which finds a balance between achieving shareholders' financial rewards and achievement in the public services. There is also a fundamental knowledge that an education system that meets society's needs as expressed through the four goals outlined in point 4 above needs a resourcing level above that apparent in 2002. The economic gains, specifically the year-on-year increase in gross domestic product (GDP) are used to provide increased funding for education as it is recognised that a primary reason for the rise in GDP is a better educated (and trained) population.

The rationale for primary education in 2015 is to provide a 'life-wide' experience, which takes account of a continued focus on formal instruction in literacy, and numeracy, together with a broadly based curriculum enacted through a rich community-based infrastructure. It is probably best described through the following diary narrative, which describes a day in the life of an 11-year-old girl, Anne, who lives in a London suburb and attends Brixhan Community Learning Park.

'Every day I travel to the learning park with my dad and my friends Katie and Narinda. We catch the tram and take two stops to our school. It only opened last year and is very large. In fact our teacher told us once that it is large enough to include the children from three schools. There are two parts to our school. One part is where we learn about numeracy and literacy, whilst the other part, the learning park is where we do all kinds of other things like humanities, art, and science. The second part is not really like a school at all, but I'll come back to that later on. When we arrive at school we have a swipe card that lets us into the classroom. Katie and Narinda go to the learning park for the morning whilst I go to my literacy and numeracy class. In the afternoon we swap round so that I go to the learning park and they go to literacy and numeracy.

The first thing I do then is to go to my class where I have the same teacher for literacy and numeracy. Almost always, there are two teachers in the classroom, one is a student teacher and the other is my regular teacher. Sometimes a teaching assistant takes us if my regular teacher has to work with the student somewhere else. When everybody's there there are 16 children in the class. We sit in a horseshoe shape. In literacy, the first thing we do is find today's lesson on our laptops. You can also see it on our computer at home so dad can find out exactly what we have been doing in class and for every class in the country some of the lesson is the same. Every lesson has a learning goal and the plan that we see shows us how the lesson is to start and gives some ideas about the middle part of the lesson for the teacher. Sometimes we do one of these things, but other times we do something different. Most of the time we work as a whole class and there are a lot of question and answer sessions between the teacher and the children. When we write, we almost always do this on our computers and often we just have to provide answers to questions that we see on our screens.

Once every few weeks, at the end of term, we have a whole week where we write a book. This is based on our work in the afternoons and we can often choose whether to do a fiction or factual piece. Overall we do five books a year, as there are five terms in the year.

After a short playtime we move on to numeracy. We have this with the same teacher who teaches us literacy. For some of this we work together as a whole class, but for other parts we all have something different on our computers. This is from our learning targets that we agreed with our teacher at the beginning of the term.

In the afternoon we go to the other part of the school which is called the learning park. This is next to where we've been in the morning and is different as some of the school is open to the public and there is also a secondary school nearby which uses some of the facilities. Sometimes we use the large public library that is mostly an electronic library. Other times we work at the museum that is attached to the school and we've also been to the art gallery. We have special access to the sports and health centre too and we go there once a week for the whole afternoon, as well as every afternoon for a week once per term. Our teacher is always telling us how lucky we are to be in this school as some other schools have to send their children to the facilities. Our classroom is in a block that is surrounded by the library, the museum, the gallery and the sports centre. Sometimes we work in our classroom, but other times we go to the learning rooms in the museum or the art gallery. We have one teaching assistant who is always with us in the afternoon, and there are also different teachers who work with us and who work in the museum, say, with members of the public. These teachers have had a different training than the teacher we have in the morning.

Every term we have a project to work on that is focused on a particular subject – humanities, science, French, arts, etc. At the beginning of the term we do some introductory work. Our teacher calls this foundation skills. When we've finished this we are given an outline for a project in the subject that we have to change so that it becomes our own. Each person in the class does something different, but our teachers help us to make sure we stick to the plan that we've agreed with her. A lot of the time we e-mail each other and our teachers to help us with our work because we don't see our teachers every day, only the teaching assistants. One of the best things that we do is called 'learning about learning'. We do this at the beginning of every term and we find out about how as individual children we like to learn. I have found out that I am better working on my own, whilst Katie learns best when there is quick-fire question and answer sessions with the teacher. At the end of these sessions we write an individual learning plan that we agree with our teacher.'

Before considering the implications for ITTE, we would like to tease out some of the main features of this vision of schooling as this will create a proper context for our later discussion.

1. Schooling takes place in the context of a community infrastructure. The school is effectively set in a learning park where there is public access to leisure and cultural facilities. There is a blurring between schooling and lifelong learning as most of the facilities of the school are also available for the community.

2. There is a clear distinction between literacy and numeracy and other areas of the curriculum. There is, as at present, a focus on the 'basics' using direct instruction. There is also however a totally different approach to other subjects. Here children have access to specialist teachers who are also community orientated. For some of the time they work with teaching assistants whose role is to facilitate and there is also a marked increase in e-communication.

3. Children have more ownership over their learning than at present. The framework for learning is still specified but, particularly in subjects beyond literacy and numeracy they are able to exercise considerable independence in relation to their learning. This is structured and agreed through individual learning plans.

4. Children are not taught by teachers all the time. In the learning park, they work with teaching assistants and have some contact with specialist subject teachers. These teachers work with the community, too, as the practice of lifelong learning has become firmly established. There is also some emphasis on e-learning. In the school, children are taught by literacy and numeracy teachers.

5. There is considerable private investment in the school and the smaller class sizes are achieved partly through the use of teaching assistants and partly through using specialist teachers who work also with the community.

All this has considerable implications for ITTE. Brixhan Community Learning Park is a professional development school. One of the staff is a full-time employee of Southwark University but whose only work is connected with ITTE students who are for large parts of their courses placed at the school in various capacities. His other responsibility is in relation to continuing professional development for all staff at the school, including for a large number of staff who are studying for masters courses.

In 2015 most ITTE is at professional-graduate level. However it involves a minimum two-year programme that includes induction. It is school based but includes a substantial amount of time considering theoretical perspectives. In the academic year 2015–16 at Brixhan, there are around 2,500 pupils from the ages of 5 to 11 years of age. There are also about 70 student teachers who have their own facilities, effectively a satellite centre to the university which is attached to the learning park. A role of the director of teacher education is to head up the programme of teacher preparation for these students, as well as leading all continuing professional development.

The curriculum for these students has responded to new research focused on learning and, in particular, meta-learning. There is a major focus in the curriculum on child development, with elements of cognitive development and the development of emotional intelligence within this. In fact it is very much the case that the study of the child is at the very centre of the curriculum. The supposition here is that unless we understand how the child learns then the development of teaching skills is happening out of context. Children's learning is a generic part of the course, but teaching skills are incorporated fully into literacy and numeracy teaching and the specialist electives that provide a foundation for those wishing to specialise in areas of the learning park. Prior to admission on to course there is a rigorous formative assessment of subject knowledge in literacy and numeracy and self–directed e-study packs for those students who have specific weaknesses in either of these areas.

The two-year, 5–11, course starts experientially with four days a week in different areas of the school and one day a week for study leave. This continues for a whole term. There is a two-week orientation course at the beginning of the course and a series of base days in the education centre throughout the term. The focus for the term is children's learning and e-distance learning materials support the study. Students spend time working with children on developing and reviewing the individual learning plans and talk with pupils in some detail about different learning styles and preferences. They observe the numeracy and literacy teaching and juxtapose this learning context with that in the learning park. They consider issues of independence and dependence in learning and begin to understand the subtleties of effective intervention in learning. They also begin to consider the impact of age on learning styles and aptitudes.

Over the next two terms, there is an in-depth focus on literacy and numeracy. As in term one, much of this takes place within the school and there is a great emphasis on actual teaching and the evaluation of this. There is also a heavy emphasis on the role of the mentor who under the guidance of the director of teacher education and as a normal, regular part of her role, works collaboratively with individual students in developing teaching skills in literacy and numeracy and then, in the education centre provides seminars and lectures for groups of students covering areas such as progression in numeracy/literacy, assessment, managing children's e-learning and behaviour management. All this is supported by a bank of nationally available materials that focus on all aspects of teaching and learning in literacy and numeracy.

As with the children, there is a strong element of individual learning and at the beginning of term two all students prepare an individual training plan that is agreed by the mentor. The individuality is expressed in different emphases within the detail of the actual teaching (e.g. for one student there may be a focus on preparing pupils for individual learning, whilst for another it may be more focused on effective teaching at the beginning of the lesson). There is also differential access to the range of supporting resources for the course. The mentor receives guidance and support from the director of teacher education and there is time for these activities including some marking of students' coursework as teaching assistants are trained to monitor classes (under national guidelines which limit any direct teaching).

A substantial bridging course between Years 1 and 2 provides students with some distance-learning material on historical and comparative educational issues. The historical development of the curriculum is considered as is the politicisation of education and research and pedagogy and policy. At the end of this students are expected to be able to articulate a provisional vision for education.

Terms one and two of Year 2 take place in the learning park. All students have the opportunity to shadow specialist teachers in the various subject areas both in their work with the pupils and with the community. Seminars and distance learning provide students with the opportunity to engage with all subject areas in the learning park and there are both strong elements of curriculum studies and subject knowledge development. During term three of Year 2, students make a decision about whether they would like to teach in the learning park or the school. There is then the equivalent of a final teaching placement and a summative judgement is made about the individual students who are then awarded QTS.

Beyond this point there is through the director of teacher education a programme of accredited continuing professional development with an expectation that a majority of teachers will study for masters degrees based on various elements of children's learning. The pedagogy of continuing professional development involves a focus on intensive base days and then supported self-study using university-provided distance-learning materials. The masters courses are based on the assumption that before theoretical perspectives can be understood readily, it is essential for there to be a context for these. The emphasis on practical teaching within initial preparation provides a rich context for the development of theoretical perspectives. All teachers have an entitlement to ten days' study leave per year and the use of teaching assistants and student teachers provides a resource to enable this to happen.

This model of teacher education may, at first sight, seem distant and unobtainable, but major elements of it are already in existence. In San Diego, California, there is a place called Balboa Park. This is a cultural focus for the city with art museums, a local history centre, concerts, natural history and so forth. There is within this a notion of 'the school in the park' where children come from a nearby inner-city school on a regular rotating basis to study art using the art museum as a stimulus and focus. The children have access to the museum and also have access to their own classroom facilities within the park. It is staffed by Museum in the Park teaching staff and by their regular teachers. Rosa Parks School is one of the schools which sends children to the Museum in the Park. At the school there is a full-time University of San Diego employee whose main job it is to manage the professional development of students in teacher preparation and experienced teachers who are studying for masters degrees. At Rosa Parks and School in the Park, there is a notion of education in the widest sense. Children have access to a broadly based curriculum which has some strikingly original elements to it. Students have access to teachers who themselves are open to professional development and are engaging with this in a deep way.

In putting forward this vision we do so partly with a sense of creativity and intrigue for the future and partly because we believe that, with a paradigm shift its piloting, or piloting of something similar, could become a reality by 2015. However we are acutely aware that there are a number of questions which provide difficult challenges for us. For example, first, could this model be applied to rural education? It implies a massive increase in the size of schools to provide viable provision for use by both the community and the children. How would this be organised in rural areas? How would the implications for small village schools be handled? How could technology help overcome such difficulties? Secondly, does the increase in resource required rule out this model being seen as a panacea for the future development of education? There are some economies at the boundary between education and heritage and with the creative use of teaching assistants, but would these be enough to offset what would probably be a large increase in required funding?

Whatever the questions and issues we argue that the kind of model outlined above should become a reality for teacher education in the twenty-first century. We note further that its realisation may not be as distant as it may seem. In this sense, it links closely to Edwards and Collison's (1996) typology of different relationships between HEIs and schools. In particular, the kind of vision we have painted has similarities with Edwards and Collison's type-3 relationship. They suggest (ibid., p. 139) that:

> 'The shift of mind that is proposed in a type-3 relationship starts from a view of education as lifelong learning which is given coherence by continuous collaboration and discussion between all providers ... Evidence of the shift of mind that is being indicated here would be, for example, collaboration in the development of planning between schools and university departments of education which attended to strategic planning, professional development and quality assurances in both sets of organisations.'

Does society have the courage to facilitate a paradigm shift in educational thinking?

References

Department for Education and Skills (DfES) (2001) *Schools: Building on Success*. London: DfEE.

Department for Education and Employment (DfEE) and Qualifications and Curriculum Authority (QCA) (1999) *The National Curriculum: Handbook for Primary Teachers in England*. London: DfEE/QCA.

Edwards, A. and Collison, J. (1996) *Mentoring and Developing Practice in Primary Schools*. Buckingham: Open University Press.

Furlong, J., Barton, L., Miles, S., Whiting, C. and Whity, G. (2000) *Teacher Education in Transition*. Buckingham: Open University Press.

Murphy, C. and Liu, M. (1998) Choices must be made: the case of education in Taiwan. *Education 3-13* 26(2):17–25.

Reynolds, D. and Farrell, S. (1996) *Worlds Apart? A Review of International Surveys of Educational Achievement Involving England*. OFSTED Reviews of Research. London: HMSO.

Wilkin, M. (1996) *Initial Teacher Training*. London: Falmer Press.

Earlier chapters in this book deal at length with a critique of the new Standards and their implementation. In this final chapter I shall try to predict what effect different visions for the future might have on individual trainee teachers. I shall present two scenarios in which I depict what life in school may be like for teachers in the future, and leave the reader to decide which of them is more likely to happen and more desirable.

Background

The new Standards for Qualified Teacher Status are the latest in a succession of documents endeavouring to raise standards in education and develop an effective teaching workforce for the twenty-first century. Debates about recruitment and retention of teachers, pupil achievement, working conditions, salary, promotion opportunities and general professional morale have dominated the education agenda. Headteachers and governors have been swept into a world of budgets, target-setting, staff appraisal and league tables. Schools are compared and contrasted on the basis of pupils' scores in national standardised tests. As Johnston (2002, p. 6) rightly comments, since the introduction of testing at the end of Key Stages, *'school organisation has changed for curricular rather than educational reasons'.* Teachers have to provide evidence of their effectiveness according to set criteria if they are to benefit from career enhancement. Parents' expectations of school have also risen dramatically and many of them scour information sources when selecting a school for their child. New technologies dominate discussions about future forms of schooling. Radical suggestions are being made about replacing the traditional one teacher to thirty pupils by purpose-built 'learning centres' containing sophisticated electronic equipment, staffed by one highly paid teacher and numerous (less well paid) assistants. For instance, the government's futuristic, 3D, computer-generated video launch coincided with the provision of free computers for 10,000 teachers (January 2002) and offers insight into what classrooms of the future might look like. These learning units will be fully carpeted and spacious rooms, free from clutter and noise, the silence broken only by the gentle tap of computer keys and the occasional gasp from highly motivated youngsters. The role of the teacher will, as Baker (2002) describes, be more akin to a Captain Kirk figure on the bridge of the Starship *Enterprise*, completing a captain's log while highly efficient classroom assistants glide past monitoring the students. If present trends continue, the 'innovation fatigue' and rapid pace of change associated with the later years of the twentieth century might soon be viewed with romantic nostalgia as a haven of peace and tranquillity!

Throughout the late 1990s and into the early part of the twenty-first century, the government has made great play of its willingness to consult with teachers and teacher trainers (educators) about proposed changes to the curriculum. Invitations for educators to comment about the proposals seem, however, to have been more about their implementation than their substance. Trainee teachers have scarcely been included in the consultation process, despite the fact that they are at the sharp end of any new initiatives affecting QTS.

Considering the plethora of new requirements and expectations imposed upon training establishments, it is remarkable that the numbers of teachers in training have been maintained. More worrying is that, according to numerous surveys, the retention rate is low, and only about half of all newly qualified teachers are in a permanent post some four or five years later. Despite the increase in the overall number of teachers (partly reflecting the increase in the school population) the issue of teacher shortages continues to be a significant issue, especially at secondary level. It is important to note that studies about the reasons for teachers leaving the profession, or not even beginning to teach, tell a consistent story: long hours, poor pupil behaviour, too much paperwork and frustration with the government's obsession with targets. A recent survey (*The Times Educational Supplement*, 2002) suggested that although about 70% of teachers enjoy most aspects of the job, workload and long hours are particularly frustrating and lead to considerable dissatisfaction.

The lists of competences to be acquired by trainees that have dominated documentation over the past decade assume that it is possible to identify and provide evidence for hundreds of 'Standards'. Critics of the system have described the classification of Standards into discrete and verifiable units as 'fragmentation' and even as 'atomisation' of the teaching process. Nevertheless, training providers have furnished trainee teachers and school mentors with booklets containing lists of criteria that trainees have to meet in order successfully to complete their school experience.

There has been an implicit assumption in earlier documentation and from government pronouncements that, providing teaching methods are satisfactory, effective learning will invariably follow. However, Pollard (2001, p. 7) has been among those to argue that policy has been *'influenced by external, economic and political factors, rather than founded on a valid understanding of how children's learning actually takes place'*.

In the *Standards for the Awards of Qualified Teacher Status* (DfES/TTA, 2002), there is a notable shift in tone, with an emphasis on the need for assessors of trainee teachers to interpret the 'guidance' with respect to the prevailing circumstances in particular schools. As evidence of this softening mood, the new document also accepts that some aspects of the Standards are likely to be stronger for some trainees than for others. In contrast to the hundreds of competences that newly qualified teachers were required to reach listed in Circular 4/98 (DfEE, 1998), the new Standards are considerably fewer in number. This synthesis is, in itself, an admission of the unsatisfactory principles on which previous attempts to define competence were based.

The second part of the Standards handbook contains numerous 'examples' to assist the development of expertise. The Foreword stresses the fact that the extra information and questions are intended to support formative assessment rather than act as a *'set of surrogate requirements'* or be *'used as a tick-list for either assessment or the design of training'* (DfES/TTA, 2002, p. 2). Previous experience suggests, however, that what begins as clarification and guidance invariably ends by being treated as if they were statutory, especially by inspection teams.

Comments made by contributors earlier in the book suggest that a number of these changes are extremely welcome, not least a move away from the barbed tone of previous documents and the baffling proposition that Standards can be applied indiscriminately in every circumstance and for every trainee teacher. Common sense about the need for a flexible interpretation of the Standards seems to have prevailed. If the government has learned from its previous mistakes and accommodated the many and varied voices that have criticised earlier versions of Standards for QTS, the prospects for future trainee teachers seem brighter. There are, none the less, a number of important issues that relate not merely to the technical completion of a training course and award of a teaching qualification, but to the personal ambition and motivation of individual trainees. Despite all the effort and finance that the government has allocated to teaching, there is still a strong sense of unease in the profession, fuelled in part by regular pronouncements by politicians that teachers must expect and accept further change. It is to the possible nature of these changes and the impact they may have upon individual trainee teachers that we now turn.

Prospects for trainee teachers

Teachers who will enrol on a course of teacher training and education during the second and third decades of this century are, in the majority of cases, just small children today. They are growing up in a world that relies increasingly upon visual images, instant forms of communication and sophisticated information sources. They will be as familiar with computers and digital technology as previous generations have been with the wireless, record player, tape recorder and video. There is a very good chance they will have regular contact with only one of their natural parents but numerous contacts with a variety of other adults in play schemes, nursery and school.

Tomorrow's trainee teachers will be widely-travelled and knowledgeable about world events. They will be immersed in a turbulence of diversity and rapid change where moral absolutes will be under constant scrutiny and challenge. On the evidence of recent trends, security cameras, security guards, security-fences and identity cards are likely to be an accepted feature of their lives. Materialism and self-interest seem destined to pervade society at the expense of self-sacrifice and community spirit.

Many questions emerge as we consider what the future holds for trainee teachers.

- What demands will be placed on them during the next 10 or 20 years?
- What will be expected of them from the government, parents and the local community?
- What factors will motivate them and what are they expecting from the job?
- How will trainees respond to the changes in educational policy and methods of schooling predicted by the present government and reflected in the Standards document?
- Will the emphasis on professional values and practice, and the more conciliatory tone of the document, enthuse prospective teachers and help to retain them?

To begin examining these questions, two scenarios are described below to offer a flavour of how someone born at the start of the twenty-first century might experience life in school as a trainee teacher sometime during the third decade. Both descriptions are set out using a similar writing 'frame' and somewhat embellished for effect, though neither of them is overstated to such an extent that they are beyond the realms of possibility.

The first scenario assumes the relentless expansion of an education system that is increasingly technologically driven. To an extent, it reflects Isaac Asimov's futuristic tale *Earth is Room Enough* (1957), set in 2055, except that in the account that follows, the future has arrived sooner than he expected! An excerpt from Asimov's tale provides a taste of the situation:

> 'Margie went into the schoolroom. It was right next to her bedroom, and the mechanical robot was on and waiting for her. It was always on at the same time every day except Saturday and Sunday, because her mother said little girls learned better if they learned at regular hours.'

Is this the future of education? What will the teacher's role become? Will technology solve the recruitment crisis and improve standards of academic attainment? Read on.

Scenario 1

Zana was born on 16 March 2000. When she first entered school as a 4-year-old in 2004, she needed a 'swipe' card to gain access. The word 'school' was in the process of being replaced by lifelong learning academies (LLAs). The length and structure of the day varied between different LLAs. Some teachers in the school were on short-term contracts, renewable annually on the basis of pupils' satisfactory examination results. By the time Zana was eight the National Curriculum had been replaced by the People's Curriculum (PC), in which 'bespoke' individualised learning programmes were provided, accessible from both school and home computers. Numerous assistant teachers or ATs (formerly teaching assistants) and a number of intern teachers or ITs (formerly trainee teachers) supervised pupils (now known as scholars) throughout the day and early evening.

When Zana left her LLA in 2018 to train as a teacher herself, institutions of higher education had become defunct and all teacher training took place on the job. A very small number of highly paid supervisory teachers (STs) had overall responsibility for ensuring that classes (now known as achievement units or AUs) functioned smoothly and that pupils met agreed learning targets. A number of scholars were adults from the local community who wished to upgrade their knowledge and qualifications. Parents and other carers (now known as home educators or HEs) monitored their children's progress and the quality of their education through the use of interactive video conferencing that facilitated home–school dialogue. Headteachers (now known as standard maintainers or SMs) oversaw a cluster of schools operating in a defined geographical area, reporting directly to the education overlord (EO), situated in Brussels.

Before Zana could be accepted on the course of training, she had to complete successfully the on-line Career Suitability Profile (CSP) to demonstrate the extent of her subject expertise. Her suitability was further assessed through use of the cerebral scan determinator (CSD), a machine that was able to probe the brain and analyse DNA to detect any personality flaws that might negate her effectiveness as a teacher.

By the time that Zana was approaching the end of her training (in 2021), a new Education Act passed through the Parliament of the Western Zone stating that scholars did not need to attend school every day, owing to the increased availability of technology in the home. All computers were voice-activated and programmed to give instant feedback. Due to the large increase in throat and voice maladies from over-speaking, the first eye-sensitive machines were being trialled. Writing had become a peripheral activity and could only be accessed through the cultural history elective. Conventionally printed books were still available from the archive room but nearly all literacy work was computerised. Monthly test results for pupils were automatically sent to a central data bank as part of the national Standards' monitoring programme. Underachieving children were required to attend the Scholar Intensification Programme (SIP) in which of the most technologically sophisticated android mentoring preceptors (AMPs) were programmed to eliminate error and inculcate effective strategies for learning. A contro-versial bill was being debated about a prototype machine capable of erasing corrupted brain cells in young children that might inhibit optimum academic attainment.

The school day did not consist of regular break times. Within certain defined limits, children were given flexibility about when they worked. Teachers did not concern themselves with the social dimensions of the scholars' development. Instead, adjustment assistants (AAs), who had been specially appointed for the purpose, catered for the affective aspects in social conformity units (SCUs). The AAs were the only members of staff allowed physically to touch children without official clearance.

There was little need for Zana to operate discipline strategies. Children were all obliged to wear behaviour rectification bracelets (BRBs), specially designed to administer a minuscule amount of chemicals into the system to counteract aggressive or inappropriate tendencies. In addition, parents and carers were anxious that their children conformed to the official requirements, as fines were automatically incurred based on the number of misdemeanours. Anyway, the gene modification programme that prepared children for prespecified employment was proving extremely successful in its 'targeted ambition' scheme.

As a trainee teacher, Zana learned how to operate the various learning systems and identify and allocate the information packages that were electronically designed for individuals. Much of her day was spent at her control console, working on a one-to-one basis with scholars requesting assistance.

In her spare time Zana enjoyed browsing through the education archives and came across pictures of classrooms from the middle of the twentieth century, where 30 children and a teacher spent most of every day in a room together. Zana shook her head in disbelief, not because of the old-fashioned desks and chairs or the lack of technology or even the strange clothing they wore, but because of the relaxed and contented looks on their faces. She contrasted these images with the austere and highly competitive environment that confronted her in the AUs and wondered what it was like to have been a trainee teacher in the old days. She came across a slogan from the end of the previous century: 'Education, education, education', and pondered how this laudable aim had been corrupted into the latest rhetoric: 'Targets, targets, targets'. However, at that point the needle on her subversion activator (SA) moved towards amber. As she did not wish to fail the training or be fined the Standard 8,000 euros for insubordination, she stopped thinking and switched her attention to the Zonal Government's latest *Top Target* publication instead.

Scenario 2

The second scenario assumes a complete rethink of educational and social priorities. It depicts an education system that incorporates the best of the old and new, mirroring another passage from Asimov (1957) in which he highlights the contrast between the futuristic world described above and school as it used to be known:

> 'The screen was lit up and it said: ''Today's arithmetic lesson is on the addition of proper fractions. Please insert yesterday's homework in the slot.'' Margie did so with a sigh. She was thinking about the old schools they had when her grandfather's grandfather was a little boy. All the kids from the whole neighbourhood came, laughing and shouting in the schoolyard, sitting together in the schoolroom, going home together at the end of the day. Margie was thinking about how the kids must have loved it in the old days. She was thinking about the fun they had.'

Zana was born on 16 March 2000. When she first entered school as a 4-year-old in 2004, she needed a 'swipe' card to gain access. The government of the day was still adamant that targets, performance and delivery were appropriate terminology for education, even when dealing with young children. There were, however, strong voices being raised about the unsuitability of treating schools like businesses and children like commodities. Teachers in the school were still on permanent contracts, but discussions with Unions included the possibility that, owing to teacher shortages, all staff should be given minimum five-year tenures. By the time Zana was eight, the National Curriculum had been replaced by a more flexible system in which primary schools could elect to devise their own programmes of study including, if parents and staff agreed, an emphasis on environmental studies and local community projects. A number of more progressive schools elected to replace timetabled slots for individual subjects with blocks of time for integrated curriculum studies, referred to as 'topic work'. The Secretary of State for Education visited a number of these progressive schools and declared that he intended to try to persuade other schools to emulate this sound educational practice. Numerous assistant teachers or ATs (formerly teaching assistants) and a number of intern teachers or ITs (formerly trainee teachers) served during regular daytime hours and, on a rota basis, during twilight hours for children with working parents.

When Zana left secondary education in 2018 to train as a teacher, institutions of higher education and local schools worked co-operatively to provide places for ITs. The divisive and unpopular practice of distinguishing between 'advanced' and 'ordinary' teachers had long been abandoned in favour of a more equitable system by which salary preferment was automatically linked with years of service. Since this egalitarian model had been introduced in 2010 there had been no staff shortages and higher morale. Adults from the local community who wished to upgrade their knowledge and qualifications were also accommodated into the teaching programmes during twilight hours only. Parents and other carers were allowed to come into school at any time of day, providing they had signed the home–school pact agreement. Headteachers reported directly to the newly formed Local Education Partnerships (LEPs). These were, according to older teachers, very similar to the concept of an LEA that had been responsible for zonal education during the last century.

Before Zana could be accepted on the course of training, she had to complete successfully the on-line Career Suitability Profile (CSP) to demonstrate the extent of her commitment to children and desire to teach. This required her to spend an hour playing with children, and an hour supervising pupils in a more formal academic setting further assessed her suitability. Observers noted her ability to interact positively with the children, her caring manner, decisive action and willingness to respond positively to advice from the regular teacher and assistants. There was unanimous agreement that Zana should be accepted on to the course.

By the time that Zana was approaching the end of her training (in 2021), she was delighted to hear that thanks to a courageous breed of cross-party politician, new guidelines were being introduced that encouraged schools to dismantle their security-cameras, razor-wire fences, intruder alarms and metal detectors. Thanks to the emphasis on social, moral and spiritual education over the past decade, behaviour in society had improved to such an extent that such contrivances were no longer considered necessary. The swing away from name, blame and shame politics towards more constructive and caring communities had paid dividends, despite sceptic voices that had prophesied doom and gloom about introducing these 'old-fashioned' Elizabethan values.

All computers were now voice-activated and programmed to give instant feedback, but due to the large increase in throat and voice maladies from over-speaking the first eye-sensitive machines were being trialled. Writing had been reintroduced as an essential activity and classes promoting neat script were extremely well attended. Conventionally printed books lined the shelves and offered a wide diversity of types. Technological information sources were available and frequently accessed, but the majority of children delighted in sharing books and reading for the sheer joy of doing so. Children's self-assessment test results had shown a big improvement since the introduction of a 'read books for pleasure' approach and away from the stifling 'systems' strategy that had been fostered on schools in the first decade of the new millennium. Underachieving children were placed in a stimulating environment in which they could explore their own interests and were encouraged to raise and solve problems. Zana could never quite understand why previous curricula had taken little or no account of the fundamental need to motivate reluctant learners by tapping into their enthusiasm and interests. She mused about the now discredited national imperatives that had disregarded this basic principle and insisted on banal conformity across every school and for every child.

The school day did not consist of regular break times. Within certain defined limits, children were given flexibility about when they worked in the computer suites, though they were obliged to attend specific instruction sessions. The special joy of school life was that all the adults in the school concerned themselves not only with academic progress but also with the social and moral dimensions of the children's development. Parents appreciated the fact that teachers and assistants were interested in their children as unique individuals. In fact, since the government had promoted the 'whole-child' approach, standards of academic achievement had risen sharply. The present Secretary of State for Education and Enjoyment had recently dubbed this new form of schooling 'child-centred education', though Zana felt sure she had heard the expression somewhere before.

There was little or no need for Zana to operate discipline strategies. Children were so keen to learn and so highly motivated that control management was hardly an issue. The newly formed nurturing family groups (NFGs) to mediate in situations of conflict had also been a positive influence. In addition, parents and carers were anxious that their children conformed to the requirements, as those who kept a clean record were given a reward of computer micro-chips at the end of each month and a special certificate to display in the 'Celebration' room.

As a trainee teacher, Zana learned how to identify children's specific needs and organise collaborative investigative projects, and she was very proud when she was awarded the 'Learning Facilitator' diploma from the zonal adviser. Much of her day was spent working alongside children as they played, explored and engaged with learning at their own level. She particularly enjoyed the flexibility that the programme allowed for children to pursue their ideas at length or turn their attention elsewhere. She felt a glow of satisfaction at how little her children abused their freedom of choice.

In her spare time Zana enjoyed browsing through the education archives and once came across pictures of classrooms around the turn of the century in which 30 children and a teacher spent much of every day in hour-long formal sessions studying 'literacy' and 'numeracy'. Zana shook her head in disbelief, not because of the old-fashioned technology or even the strange clothing they wore, but because of the intense and anxious looks on so many faces. She was puzzled about the way politicians had, against advice, insisted on the imposition of a deadening curriculum structure that stifled creativity, broke the hearts of many teachers and led to the first and only national teachers' strike in 2005. She contrasted the austere and competitive environment of 20 years before with the relaxed but purposeful learning environment in which she presently worked. She came across an old propaganda slogan from the turn of the century: 'Those who can, teach', and contrasted the dreadful teacher shortages of those days with the flood of people now wishing to do the job. However, she broke off her musings as the local training co-ordinator had popped in to see her with £8,000 of housing credit to celebrate her success in being granted full teacher status.

Motivating trainee teachers

Neither of the above scenarios is intended to be a prediction about the situation in schools some 20 years from now. What they do, however, is to highlight the fact that different educational priorities provide for a variety of challenges and expectations that impinge upon the work of trainees and qualified teachers. In the first scenario, technology has been exploited to raise the achievement levels of all children. In the second scenario, technology takes a subordinate role, and care for the social, moral and spiritual dimensions is commensurate with academic progress. In the first scenario the current trends of testing, benchmarking and strict government control continue to dominate the agenda. In the second scenario, the emphasis has switched to a more liberal view of education with echoes of the integrated learning style that characterised the 1960s and 1970s. In the first scenario, the trainee teacher is expected to conform strictly to an imposed and closely monitored curriculum. In the second scenario trainees who demonstrate an empathy with children and nurturing qualities are commended, the curriculum is less intensive and schools have greater freedom of choice over their priorities.

Experienced teachers working in schools in the 2020s will have been trained during the late 1990s and been immersed in a prevailing belief that formal lessons in literacy and numeracy, with strictly imposed time constraints, are necessary and desirable. They will have lived through the introduction of computer technology, target-setting, performance-related pay, thresholds, fast-track promotions and the relegation of foundation subjects in the curriculum. These experienced teachers will have been pounded by rhetoric from politicians, confused by the contradiction between expressions of outrage about low standards of achievement, and the debt that the nation owes to teachers' professional commitment. They will have felt the tension and terror of inspections, spent sleepless nights worrying about the percentage of their classes that reach particular levels of attainment in national tests, and sighed with relief when tests were over and they were able to stop 'coaching' the children for a while. Experienced teachers will have seen their salaries increase quite sharply and been able to delegate some of the more mundane tasks to assistants. However, they will have noted the concomitant increase in paperwork and accountability to parents, governors and the headteacher. The job will seem to have become less about the pleasure of working with children (though this will always be of prime importance to them) and more about responding to a variety of directives. Only a few teachers at the start of the third decade will sigh wistfully and speak in dulcet tones about the 'good old days', particularly as nearly all of them will have left the profession before the age of 50.

New teachers joining the profession during the second and third decades of the new century will be 'children of their age', adopting or accommodating most of the conventions of the time. It is impossible to predict with certainty the variety of changes they will meet, though an increasing use of technology appears irresistible. The ubiquitous comment from politicians that we are living in a time of change and must adapt our methods to take account of this reality is undeniable. It is equally true, however, that the world has *always* been experiencing a time of change. Although the pace has undoubtedly been extremely rapid in respect of technological sophistication, communication methods and access to information, yet many features of human behaviour and desire are more constant. We can, therefore, gain some insight into what will remain important for teachers in every era by a consideration of the *motivating factors* that have been, and remain, strongly influential in a person's decision to teach.

Research by Reid and Caudwell (1997), Johnston *et al.* (1999), Donnelly (2000) and others suggests that in large measure people are motivated to teach because they enjoy working with children and young people, and like helping them to develop their full potential. Spear *et al.* (2000), in their wide-ranging review of factors motivating and demotivating prospective and practising teachers, concluded that the top three influences were working with children, good relationships with colleagues, and the development of warm, personal relationships with pupils. A study by Hayes (2000) indicated that primary teachers are motivated by the desire to work with children in a happy school environment, and relish the enjoyment that comes from teaching them. Trainee teacher respondents considered teaching to be a worthwhile job and relished the thought they could contribute something of value to society by positively influencing the children they taught. In this regard, Silcock (1999) argues that, despite the dismissal of the child-centred philosophy by central government, primary school teachers' commitment to it may have been right after all. He concludes that if politicians were more willing to trust the soundness of teachers' professional judgement, higher standards would be achieved than is possible through the present 'top-down' attempts to drive through improvements by means of unwelcome reforms.

In common with other jobs, teaching is an amalgam of good and frustrating features, as Thody *et al.* (2000, p. 84) remind us:

> *'At bad times the teacher's job can seem to be a constant round of aggravation with awkward colleagues, demanding parents, detached senior management and pupils from hell. To deal with conflicts with these, we need to keep a sense of balance. Re-member that our schools are also full of warmth, with friendly, helpful colleagues, co-operative pupils and supportive parents.'*

However, it is beyond dispute that many of the key factors that provide the initial spur for becoming a primary teacher are rooted in the affective and social domain: caring, fulfilment and impact upon society. By contrast, trainee primary teachers' enthusiasm is adversely affected by the assessment and bureaucratic demands placed upon them. As Humphreys and Hyland (2002, p. 8) rightly claim, *'there is a tendency for the rationalist and reflective practice models of teaching to overlook the affective and conative domains.'* For trainee teachers, the only place where they gain immediate access to this 'affective fulfilment' is on school placement. If school experience is unfulfilling, no other course benefits (such as getting a degree) or aspirations (such as the thought of ultimate job security) adequately compensate.

In acknowledging the factors that motivate trainee teachers, it is worth being aware of a paradox. While on the one hand it is important to attract good-quality applicants, it is equally essential to make sure that their idealism is balanced by the realities of being a teacher (Evans, 1997; Chambers and Roper, 2000). If students begin a training course with a rose-tinted view of the job, their idealism is sure to be tarnished somewhat after experiencing the challenges, as well as the joys, of a teacher's working life (Hayes, 2001a). Finding a balance between retaining idealism and exposing trainee teachers to the intensity of the job presents one of the main challenges for the future.

The impact of the training curriculum 2002

The 2002 Standards for newly qualified teachers suggest that politicians may have started to take seriously the concerns expressed about the adverse effects of earlier statutory requirements. The fragmentation of teaching into hundreds of separate competences, each of which could (in principle) be confirmed through the provision of evidence, appears to have been replaced by a more sensible framework of expectations. It is encouraging to see a direct acknowledgement that teaching is not to be regarded as a mechanistic exercise in which children's learning is ensured merely by applying the appropriate teaching technique. There is also a fairly strong sense in the new document that previous bombastic rhetoric to the effect that well structured teaching would inevitably yield high standards of achievement, regardless of the school situation, has been replaced by a more considered tone.

Politicians claim that, thanks to their rigorous policies, standards of teaching and pupil achievement have risen. They are both correct and mistaken in this assertion. They are *correct* in as much as, broadly speaking, a larger percentage of children have gained higher levels in national tests. Many teachers have welcomed the structure provided by the National Numeracy Strategy and adapted the Literacy Strategy to suit their situation. There has been a general welcome for the impact of information and communication technology (ICT) in schools and standards in some poor schools have been dramatically improved. They are *mistaken* in failing to recognise that there has been a price to pay in achieving some of these results, such as the following.

- The demise of what was formerly known as 'creative writing'. Primary children have had much less opportunity to develop writing other than within the ubiquitous 'writing frames'.
- The reduction in collaborative forms of inquiry, problem-solving and investigations in mathematics and science as they have been considered too time-consuming. Instead, experiments are tightly controlled by the teacher, who is dominated by the need to meet predetermined 'learning objectives'.
- The loss of cross-curricular projects, the best of which provided opportunities for children to pursue their interests enthusiastically.
- The marginalising of subjects outside the core.
- The curtailment of teachers' creativity and spontaneity as they have struggled to conform to 'guidelines' and prepare for inspection.
- The early retirement and resignation of thousands of good teachers, and the low morale amongst many others.

Of course, these 'costs' do not apply to every situation. Some schools have managed to respond to government expectations while incorporating a range of exciting and innovative curriculum initiatives into the programme. Others have bravely confronted the obvious limitations of national policy decisions or exploited them to the children's advantage. Yet others have been intimidated by the harsh consequences of resistance and meekly conformed (Hayes, 2001b).

The shape of things to come

So how will the changes in the education agenda over recent years and the tone of the most recent Standards document affect the aspirations of future trainee teachers? At the heart of the debate is the issue of how the role of the teacher should be defined or, rather, how the numerous roles that teachers fulfil should be prioritised. If prospective teachers embark on a training course in the belief that they are entering a profession dedicated to the development of young minds through innovative and child-centred ideas, only to discover that most of the teaching is constrained by external demands, it is little wonder they become disillusioned. If they embark on their training in the belief that a sizeable proportion of the teacher's work is dedicated to the social and moral development of children, only to discover that the role is largely one of imparting knowledge and monitoring test results, no one should be surprised by their loss of motivation. If they enter the profession in the belief that they will be free to use their creativity, personality and intuition to inject a sense of purpose into the classroom, only to discover that time constraints, fear of inspection and obsession with targets dominates the agenda, their negative reactions can be forecast.

The future is not predictable but neither is it inevitable. Politicians have their say and try hard to have their way, but parents, teachers and prospective teachers who care deeply about children's education and welfare must ensure that governments who become inflated with their own importance are given short thrift. Hargreaves and Fullan (1998, pp. 56–57) put the issue into perspective:

> 'Teaching, of course, is charged with emotion, positively and negatively. It is a passionate vocation. Good teachers are not just well oiled machines. Computers can never replace them. They are emotional, passionate beings who fill their work and their classes with pleasure, creativity, challenge and joy.'

Every aspiring teacher is a bit dewy-eyed about the job but it remains to be seen whether the 2002 Standards offer the first tentative steps towards a teaching profession that Zana and her contemporaries will be pleased to embrace. The signs, however, are promising.

References

Asimov, I. (1957) *Earth is Room Enough*. Garden City, NY: Doubleday.

Baker, M. (2002) Futuristic schools, but Victorian staffing. BBC Education website, 12 January (http://news.bbc.co.uk/hi/english/education/features/mikebaker).

Chambers, G. N. and Roper, T. (2000) Why students withdraw from initial teacher training. *Journal of Education for Teaching*, 26(1): 25–43.

Department for Education and Employment (DfEE) (1998) *Teaching: High Status, High Standards*. Circular 4/98. London: DfEE.

Department for Education and Skills (DfES) and Teacher Training Agency (TTA) (2002) *Qualifying to Teach: Professional Standards for Qualified Teacher Status and Requirements for Initial Teacher Training*. London: DfES/TTA.

Donnelly, J. (2000) All the right reasons? *Managing Schools Today*, 9(5): 37–39.

Evans, L. (1997) Understanding teacher morale and job satisfaction. *Teaching and Teacher Education* 13(8): 831–45.

Hargreaves, A. and Fullan, M. (1998) *What's Worth Fighting for in Education?* Buckingham: Open University Press.

Hayes, D. (2000) *Motivation for Teaching: a Questionnaire Survey among BEd Student Primary Teachers*. Plymouth: Rolle School of Education, University of Plymouth.

Hayes, D. (2001a) Don's diary: a life in the day of a primary teacher. *Curriculum* 22(1): 2–16.

Hayes, D. (2001b)Professional status and an emerging culture of conformity amongst teachers in England. *Education 3–13*, 29(1): 43–49.

Humphreys, M. and Hyland,T. (2002) Theory, practice and performance in teaching: professionalism, intuition and jazz. *Educational Studies* 28(1): 5–15.

Johnston, J. (2002) The changing face of teaching and learning. In J. Johnston *et al.* (eds.) *Teaching the Primary Curriculum*. Buckingham: Open University Press.

Johnston, J., McKeown, E. and McEwan, E. (1999) Primary teaching as a career choice: the views of male and female sixth-form students. *Research Papers in Education* 14(2): 181–97.

Pollard, A. (2001) Towards a new perspective on children's learning. In C. Richards (ed.) *Changing English Primary Education: Retrospect and Prospect*. Stoke-on-Trent: Trentham Books.

Reid, I. and Caudwell, J. (1997) Why did secondary PGCE students choose teaching as a career? *Research in Education* 58: 46–58.

Silcock, P. (1999) *New Progressivism*. London: Falmer Press.

Spear, M., Gould, K. and Lee, B. (2000) *Who Would be a Teacher?* Slough: NFER.

Thody, A., Gray, B. and Bowden, D. (2000) *The Teacher's Survival Guide*. London: Continuum.

The Times Educational Supplement (2002) Happy in the job, despite the hours. No. 4466: 4–5.

This book has focused on the major themes that have emerged during the consultation and development period of *Qualifying to Teach*. It has hence considered issues such as the importance of inclusion, professional values and practice, new approaches to partnership and the role and place of subject specialism. All these issues permeate new programmes leading to the award of Qualified Teacher Status. All are important and providers are required to ensure that their arrangements reflect these fully.

Yet embedded within the document is a requirement that has the potential to revolutionise the initial teacher training and education sector. Its significance has become more and more apparent during 2001-2002. Requirement 2.3 states, quite simply, that all providers must 'ensure that training takes account of individual training needs' (DfES/TTA (2002), p.15). The potential implications of this are far-reaching.

At one extreme of a spectrum, training could, over a period of time, become essentially individual. Trainees, following graduation, would arrive on programmes having already achieved some of the Standards. They would in essence bring their undergraduate credits to a provider and an individual training plan would be negotiated. This would lead to exemption from large parts of the programme and individual tracking would ensue. Flexible/modular provision would become centre stage as its ethos and concept permeated all routes of initial teacher training and education (ITTE). The benefits of this vision would include widening access, faster recruitment to the profession and an enhanced recognition of the importance of differentiation in ITTE. The downside (potentially) involves the expensive management of individualised training, a fragmentation of any training culture and the danger of an impression being created which suggests training to teach is rather unproblematic.

At the other end of the spectrum, training would need to have enhanced elements of individuality, achieved through increased numbers of options and electives on full-time undergraduate and postgraduate programmes, an enhanced place being given to professional objective setting and differentiation within courses.

We would argue that individualised training is a reality in the new era of ITTE particularly given its place in the new OFSTED methodology. It may well help the recruitment of more teachers to the profession as access will be widespread. Whether the quality of new teachers and their commitment to the profession will be enhanced in a profound sense is yet to be seen. The danger of individualisation is that it creates a culture where learning to teach is perceived as 'too quick and easy'. The potential of individualisation is to ensure that gifted and able people enter the profession who would otherwise have been barred. Balancing the danger and potential will be a major challenge for providers.

Neil Simco and Tatiana Wilson